The Living Book of Nature

Translated from the French
Original title: LES SECRETS DU LIVRE DE LA NATURE

Prosveta S.A – B.P.12 – 83601 Fréjus CEDEX (France)
ISSN 0763-2738
ISBN 2-85566-396-2
original edition: ISBN 2-85566-291-5

Omraam Mikhaël Aïvanhov

The Living Book of Nature

Izvor Collection — No. 216

P R O S V E T A

TABLE OF CONTENTS

Readers are asked to note that Omraam Mikhaël Aïvanhov's teaching was exclusively oral. This volume includes passages from several different lectures all dealing with the same theme.

Chapter 1

THE LIVING BOOK OF NATURE

From time immemorial philosophers have recognized in man a miniature universe. In the temples of antiquity he was portrayed as the key to the door of the Great King's palace, because all that exists in the universe, whether it be energy or matter, exists to a lesser degree in man. So the universe is known as the macrocosm (the great world) and man as the microcosm (the small world.) And 'God' is simply the name man has given to the sublime Spirit who created both worlds, the great and the small, who breathes life into them, maintaining them in existence.

Created in order to live and develop, man, the microcosm, must necessarily maintain a permanent bond with Nature, the macrocosm. He must be constantly tuned in, a partner in a continuous relationship of exchange. It is this interaction, this symbiosis between man and Nature that we call Life. Life is nothing more than a ceaseless flow of give-and-take between man and Nature, and sickness and death follow if this flow is interrupted or obstructed. The food we eat and drink, the air we breathe, are God's own life. There is nothing in the whole Cosmos that is not animated by the Divine Spirit of God. All things created live and breathe. All things pulsate in communion with that boundless flow of life streaming from the Godhead, penetrating the furthest reaches of Creation, from the greatest star to the most minute particle of matter. As St. Paul says, 'In Him we live and breathe and have our being.'

This is symbiosis and it is the key to life. Health and sickness, beauty and ugliness, wealth and poverty, intelligence and stupidity, all are determined by the quality of our relationship with Nature. For everything is nourishment, respiration, ceaseless interchange. When we eat we make an exchange in the physical world, our feelings and emotions are an exchange on the astral plane and when we use our minds it is an exchange on the mental plane. Why do so many people suffer from obstructions of one kind or another in their bodies? Simply because they eat or breathe in such a way that the normal flow of exchange between themselves and Nature is obstructed and as a result they fall ill. The pattern is the same for our hearts and minds. If our minds are closed to the light, if our hearts contain no warmth, if we do not throw out negative thoughts and feelings, like so much rubbish, then our minds and hearts suffocate and die.

If you want to live in a constant state of contentment and joy you have to learn how to live this symbiotic relationship with Nature correctly. Above all, you must open your hearts to Nature and feel your mutual bonds, feel that you are a part of Nature. When you open your heart to the divine current flowing through the universe you are establishing the perfect relationship of exchange, a totally new intelligence begins to awaken within you and you begin to grasp even the most subtle philosophical thoughts. Perhaps your friends will say, 'Did you know that such and such a philosopher says what you have just said?' No, you did not know. And you do not need to know. All you know with complete certainty is this relationship of exchange because you live it and feel it in your whole being. No doubt it is excellent to be able to quote the wisdom of philosophers but it is far better to be able to give proof of their wisdom from your own experience. Instead of reading a lot of books, therefore, it is better to establish a bond with the only truly inexhaustible, immortal source: Nature. Instead of drawing quotations from the books of men – for all men die and, because of their imperfections, all are in error to some degree – from now on we should quote only from the great living Book of Nature. It is the only book that contains all truth, for only Nature is eternally true and trustworthy.

A great Master or Initiate is someone who understands exactly how man is built, and who has an intimate knowledge of the whole of Nature. He can, therefore, explain how man should exchange with Nature through his thoughts, feelings and actions. Orientals say that you can learn more by spending five minutes with a genuine Master than in twenty years in the best universities of the world. A Master can teach you the science of Life, for a great Master possesses true Life.

The major difference between what you learn at a university and what you learn in an initiatic school is that a university can teach you everything about the superficial, exterior aspects of life, everything, that is, except life itself. After years and years of studying at a university you find yourself exactly as you were when you began. with the same faults and failings. True, you have perhaps become a very distinguished scholar. You have learned to use complicated instruments, to quote from many different authors, to use your tongue to great effect and even to earn a great deal of money. But your ability to have a harmful influence on other people's minds has also increased. Whereas if you study Initiatic Science you will soon find that a profound transformation is taking place: you become more discerning, morally stronger, and you begin to have a beneficial influence on others.

Studying at a university is like dissecting and analysing a fruit in a physics or chemistry laboratory. You can find out exactly what the skin, the flesh, the seeds and the juice contain in terms of physical elements but you do not really taste and experience the fruit or feel its effect upon you unless you use the natural instruments God has given you. Initiatic Science will certainly not teach you anything about the physical structure of the fruit but it will teach you how to eat it and soon you will feel all the wheels within you beginning to spin more smoothly. Then you will be able to apply yourself to studying the Book of Nature. The chemical, physical and astronomical aspects are explained far more fully and exactly than in any university text and you will discover how they are all linked and interrelated.

It is certainly very useful to study various disciplines deeply. Each one reveals a different aspect of the universe and of life. But modern scientific methods are such that they can only study what is dead. One day people will begin to realize that science needs to have life breathed into it, that it must be applied to all aspects of reality. Once this is understood, mathematical formulae, for example, or geometric forms and properties will begin to speak in other accents and men will discover that the same laws govern our thoughts, feelings and actions. This is what I mean by true Science. At the moment we know too much about astronomy, anatomy and mathematics: but no one ever sees the connection between them. Above all, no one ever links the sciences with the nature and life of man.

Let me give you an example: you are under the impression that addition, subtraction, division and multiplication hold no more secrets for you. But in fact you will never understand what addition is if you do not know that it is the heart that adds. The heart only knows how to add. It adds and adds. In fact it often adds so many things together that it gets everything all mixed up! And the intellect subtracts. Multiplication is an activity of the soul, whereas division is an activity of the spirit. It will help you to understand this if you see how human beings behave at different stages of their lives. A baby, for instance, needs to touch everything. He picks up everything he can lay hands on and puts it in his mouth: childhood is governed by the heart It is a time for adding. In adolescence this changes: a child's intellect becomes more active and he has a tendency to reject whatever he perceives as useless, harmful or unpleasant. In other words, he subtracts. Later, in adulthood, he will begin to multiply. His life will be filled with women, children and houses, his business expands and he acquires possessions of all kinds. And finally, when he is old, he begins to think about leaving for the next world: he makes his will and distributes his belongings. He has reached the stage of division.

So we start by accumulating and then, later, we discard much of what we have accumulated. The good things must be planted and tended so that they multiply, and if you do not know how to plant your thoughts and feelings, then you know nothing about true multiplication. If you know how to plant correctly you can expect to reap a rich harvest which you can then divide up and distribute to others. We are constantly in a position where we need to apply one of these mathematical operations to our lives. When we are feeling heavy-hearted, for instance, we must subtract, that is, get rid of our sadness. Sometimes we should refuse to subtract, if our intellect tries to persuade us to discard a true friend under the pretext that he is not socially or intellectually distinguished. Sometimes we multiply bad things and neglect to plant good things. So you see, if we really want to understand the four basic mathematical operations we should begin by studying their application to our lives. Later we can learn to go on to squares, square roots, logarithms and so on. But, for the time being, we must be content with the four basic operations because we have still not learned to add and subtract correctly. Sometimes people 'add' themselves to an inveterate ne'er-do-well, or 'subtract' from their hearts and minds good intentions or high ideals because some chance acquaintance has convinced them that high ideals only lead to death from starvation!

Everything around us, even our everyday needs and apparently insignificant acts, all have profound meaning. Our most commonplace gestures can reveal important secrets if we learn to decode them. The Master Peter Deunov used to say, 'Nature entertains ordinary people and instructs disciples but she reveals her secrets only to the wise.' Everything in Nature possesses form, content and meaning. The form is for the common man, the content for the disciple and the hidden meaning for the wise, for Initiates.

Nature is the great book that we must learn to read. Nature is the great cosmic powerhouse with which we must make contact. And if we ask how this can be done, the answer is very simple: the secret is love. If we love Nature because it is God's masterpiece and not merely for our own pleasure and amusement, a hidden spring within us will begin to well up and cleanse us of all our impurities, clear away all obstructions and establish a flow of exchange thanks to which we shall receive knowledge and understanding. As soon as love enters into the picture, living beings and even inanimate objects open up like flowers. If we love Nature she will speak to us from within for we are a part of her.

Jacob Boehme, the great German mystic, earned his living as a cobbler. Suddenly one day he saw everything in a light so brilliant he could not bear it. Everything he laid eyes on seemed to be lit from within. No doubt he had earned that privilege in an earlier life! In a panic he ran out of his house and fled into the countryside, but there it was stronger still: everything, the stones, the trees, the flowers and the grass all seemed to be made of light and to speak to him out of that light! Many clairvoyants and mystics have had similar experiences and they know that all of Nature is alive and filled with light.

Gradually, as our perception of Nature changes, we change our destiny. If we consider Nature as something lifeless we diminish the life within us. If we realize that Nature is alive then we shall have a share in the life of everything Nature contains: the earth, plants, animals, even the stars, and the power of the living Spirit within us will be increased and intensified.

Chapter 2

DAY AND NIGHT

I

Nature has a life all its own, a life which takes a multiplicity of forms. The weather is just one example: clear skies, rain, fog and snow are all manifestations of the life of Nature. The four seasons with all the visible transformations that accompany the passage from spring to summer, from summer to autumn and winter, are Nature's language, and it is up to us to learn it. Day follows night, activity alternates with repose, wakefulness with sleep: in every area of life we find this pattern of ebb and flow. Day represents activity, night is repose. Of course, at night while we are asleep there is work going on of a different kind, not on the conscious level but in the subconscious.

Day corresponds to consciousness and night to the subconscious. Day is wakefulness, night is sleep. Day is activity, night is passivity. Day is the time for output and expenditure (for all activity implies expenditure of some kind), whereas night is the time for refuelling and recuperation. No one can go on spending indefinitely without replenishing supplies and recharging his batteries. But before you can be recharged you have to be cleansed, and this is what takes place at night in the subconscious. The night-time activity of the subconscious is directly related to certain other functions and, primarily, to that of cleansing. Harmful, toxic elements accumulated during the day are dissipated and the respiratory, circulatory and eliminative tracts are cleared to allow the free flow of all the body fluids.

The need to be wide awake and active calls for a considerable expenditure of matter and energy. You cannot imagine how much energy the brain uses just to maintain a state of consciousness. Simply staying awake uses up a fantastic amount of energy! And if the materials and energy your brain needs to stay awake are in short supply during the day, you will have to replenish them by sleeping, if only for a few minutes. Often, two or three minutes are enough to recharge one's batteries and restore energy.

Day and night, activity and repose, consciousness and subconsciousness, this is the pattern that marks men's lives and everything in creation. Spring and summer are day; autumn and winter are night. During the night Nature slumbers and replenishes its supplies of energy so that when spring and summer come round again it can produce fruit once more. The centre of activity of a tree or any other plant moves up and down, from one level to another with the seasons. In autumn and winter it is the roots which are hard at work while activity ceases in the trunk and branches: leaves, flowers and fruit wither and fall to the ground. This is the subconscious phase. In spring and summer the activity moves to a higher level which corresponds to the level of consciousness and in autumn, once again, the centre of activity moves downwards, and so it goes on.

The alternation of day and night can be seen, too, in the span of a month: while the moon waxes it is day – a day which lasts two weeks – and while it wanes it is night – another two weeks. When the moon is waxing, the centre of human activity moves upwards to the brain and people are more energetic, active and productive. When the moon is on the wane, the centre of activity moves down again to the stomach and sexual organs. People are less vigorous on the mental, conscious level and more so on the sensual, subconscious level. They are inclined to eat and to sleep more. So a month is divided into two weeks of day and two weeks of night. Within a period of twenty-four hours, too, there can be an alternation of day and night several times and, similarly, even within a single hour.

Day, therefore, connotes wakefulness, activity and expenditure, but if there were no night in which to prepare it, there would be no day. As an example, take the period of gestation which precedes birth: for nine months a baby lives in the dark night of his mother's womb. He can see nothing, is conscious of nothing. Nor can he be seen. Only his mother can feel him moving, a little, from time to time. So human life begins with a night that lasts nine months followed by a day that lasts ninety years! And throughout the long day of life, other, shorter days and nights alternate ceaselessly, but of course you realize that all this is symbolic.

In the Book of Genesis it says, 'And the evening and the morning were the first day... and the evening and the morning were the second day.' 'The evening' means night. 'The morning means day. Perhaps you wonder why God began with night. Simply bemuse, as I have already said, if there were no night there would be no day. Night prepares the way for day. Day prepares nothing: it is spendthrift, it even wastes what has been stored up during the night. Before the sun, moon and stars appeared in the heavens, there was a period of preparation in the obscurity and darkness of night. Initiatic Science teaches that it is night that precedes and prepares the way for day, darkness for light. Take a piece of coal, for example: it is completely black and lifeless. But its blackness is only a prelude to the bright flame which will soon pierce that obscurity. So, darkness comes first. And from darkness light is born because darkness is the necessary preparation before light can emerge.

Darkness represents unorganized, formless matter, the obscure activity of the subconscious before the emergence of any kind of conscious light or understanding. But it is not enough to know this in theory: we need to learn how to put these notions to practical use. When the sky is overcast and the sun hidden, then is the time to let the subconscious do its work. On other days, when the sun is shining and the weather and electromagnetic currents are conducive to work on the conscious or even the superconscious level, then you can use a different approach. But you must learn to adapt to circumstances and change your level of activity. A dull, overcast day corresponds to night and you should put a stop to your mental activity and work with the solar plexus, on a lower level.

The solar plexus is the seat of the subconscious whereas consciousness resides in the brain. The subconscious is linked to the whole cosmos, to the immensity of the universe. It represents the collective aspect of being, so that when you move onto this level you are plunged into the ocean of universal life. You are linked to and become one with the current of life which courses through the cosmos. By means of your solar plexus you vibrate in rhythm with the immensity of creation. When you want to be a conscious, free and isolated individual again you have to move back to the level of the brain, for the brain has the capacity to individualize us whereas the solar plexus has the capacity to restore us to the collectivity: the work of the solar plexus is a nocturnal work.

During the day you are an individual. You recognize yourself as separate from others and sometimes even opposed and hostile to others. But when you sleep you have no individual life any more. You merge into the life of the universe, you melt into the immensity of the cosmos and from it you draw the reserves, the sustenance you need to restore your strength, just like a fish feeding on the elements dissolved in the waters of the ocean. Human beings emerge from and then dive back into the cosmic ocean, and this alternating movement is what we call day and night, consciousness and subconsciousness, wakefulness and sleep.

Darkness, therefore, comes before light. The ancient alchemists understood this, and when they speak of 'light emerging from darkness' it means that light is the fruit of the long, preparatory work which has taken place in obscurity. But if it is possible to work in darkness and obscurity, does this not mean, in fact, that there is no such thing as absolute darkness? The night is lit by a dazzling light, but it is an astral light which is invisible to our physical eyes. Darkness for some is light for others. Darkness and light coexist at one and the same time.

You might say that light is the daughter of darkness. The child, after all, emerges from the womb of its mother, not the other way around. Light is incapable of giving birth to obscurity, on the contrary, light dissipates obscurity. But obscurity gives birth to light. How this can be is a mystery: the mystery of movement. Without movement there is no light. First of all there has to be friction, abrasion and movement which produce heat, and the heat is then transformed into light. And if you transpose this on to the human level you can say that it is the will that produces movement, movement produces heat, that is love, and as love intensifies it pours itself out in the form of light, that is intelligence and wisdom.

So the beginning is the will, a movement. The will is something dark and obscure. The will dwells in darkness. Its work is hidden, an unseen activity which produces heat. The heat, too, is unseen but it can be felt and as the heat intensifies, light begins to appear. This is exactly what took place at Creation. Genesis says, 'And the spirit of God moved upon the face of the waters.' 'The waters' represents the formless matter fashioned by the Spirit of the Lord in His work of creation. The moving of the Spirit produced heat and the heat was transformed into light, revealed by the words, 'Let there be light.' God created the world through will (movement), love (heat) and wisdom (light). And man has the power to create in the same way, for movement dwells in the solar plexus in the form of life, heat in the heart in the form of love, and light in the mind in the form of wisdom. And we see the same pattern portrayed in the Hindu Triad: Brahma, Vishnu and Siva. The Indian Rishis who had penetrated the secret depths of creation placed Brahma (the Creator) in the solar plexus, Vishnu (the Preserver) in the heart and Siva (the Destroyer) in the brain. As you can see, there is so much here that needs to be studied in depth!

II

There are, as it were, two worlds: the world of light in which everything is clearly visible, where shapes and colours, dimensions and distances can all be seen and danger can be avoided in the light of day. Then there is the world of darkness in which all these realities fade and are concealed by other realities. And human beings, who begin by spending a nine-month-long night in their mothers' wombs before confronting the world, go through life repeating this pattern, alternately awake and emerging into light, or asleep and returning to the dark of night. In his account of the Creation in the Book of Genesis, Moses says, 'And the evening and the morning...' because, from the esoteric point of view, evening or night-time comes before the visible manifestation of day.

Manifestation is daytime, whereas the time of preparation and construction, the time for bringing form out of chaos and obscurity is night. Night always precedes day and the most important realities always take shape, initially, in the dark. This being so, how is it that esoteric philosophy also equates night with the forces of evil and day with the forces of good? Why is darkness seen as a symbol of Hell and wickedness, whereas light symbolizes Heaven and good? In fact they are only one facet of what they symbolize, a very limited, albeit truthful aspect.

When the sun gets up in the morning it illuminates a limited area in space and on earth and everything within that area can be clearly seen: you can learn from what is around you, see where you are going, work and measure shapes and sizes and investigate reality. But when the sun goes down and the shape and colour of objects are no longer clearly visible, you begin to see the infinite space above you and the myriad stars in the night sky. The vision is so immense, so vast, it can go to your head like wine. Your soul takes flight and soars away, losing itself and fusing with other beings in that immensity. A feeling of peace and serenity takes hold of you, for in the face of such immensity, such majesty, many petty difficulties fade into nothing and you melt into the life of the universe.

Do we have to belittle the importance of the sun simply because there are other suns in the universe? No, not at all. But we do have to study Nature's language and understand the role of the sun. The role of the sun is to individualize us. It gives us the light we need to learn and to work at our evolution. If the sun were not there this would be impossible, we would lose ourselves in the immensity of the cosmos. For man to become individualized and fully conscious the sun is absolutely indispensable.

The sun, the moon and the stars are all represented within us. The sun is in our minds in the form of light and in our feelings in the form of love. In our bodies it is represented by the heart, the centre and fountainhead from which flows the blood which nourishes our organs, just as the sun nourishes the planets. But the real centre of our physical life is the solar plexus, for that is where life originates. The Russians call this part of the body *jivot* and in Bulgarian, *jivot* means life. For the Russians, *jivot* designates the region of the belly: stomach, solar plexus and abdomen, and we learn from the Gospels that when man becomes a true temple of the living God, his belly will become 'a well of water springing up to eternal life.' Living waters flow from the solar plexus through the umbilical cord, bringing life and nourishment to the unborn child.

The sun symbolizes the intellect because it is our intellect that throws light onto reality and enables us to see and understand things. Without the light of the intellect we would be blind, and the blind can so easily go astray and get lost. The intellect represents our inner sun in the form of understanding and comprehension, clarity and wisdom, although, in our present state of evolution, it does not always enlighten us very well.

Like the sun, the role of the intellect is to individualize us, to set us off from the mass, from cosmic immensity, and make us conscious and capable of learning. So it is a very useful tool. But, at the same time, it severs us from true reality: cosmic immensity. This is why Hindus call the intellect the Destroyer of reality. Yes, the intellect 'destroys' reality because it hides it from us, exactly as the sun prevents us from seeing the immensity of space and other stars and allows us to see only a small corner of this earth.

The intellect, especially in its present-day manifestations in the work of many thinkers, philosophers and scientists, is the assassin of reality. It is their intellect which prevents many scholars from seeing and grasping the essence of reality, and the more they rely on their intellect the more completely do they cut themselves off from the cosmos and its immensity. One may well wonder if this state of affairs is going to last for ever, but I can assure you it will not. In the plan of

Cosmic Intelligence the present development of the intellect is only a phase. It was inevitable that in developing his intellect man would, at the same time, cut himself off from the whole and end by falling into materialism, unbelief and even atheism. But at the same time, Cosmic Intelligence knows full well that this state of affairs will not last. The lower intellect which is so attached to lifeless, mechanical, frozen aspects of Nature, is linked to the higher intellect, the causal body.

I expect you remember the diagram of man and his six bodies: physical, astral, lower mental, higher mental or causal, buddhic and atmic. In the centre are the two mental levels: the lower mental body or *manas* as the theosophists call it, and the higher mental or causal body, and the two are closely linked. In the long run, the activity of the lower level will awaken the higher mental level. An intellect which enables man to develop as an individual and to master the material world is a necessity. If he were totally immersed in the collective, universal dimension of life he would be incapable of influencing material creation. This is the danger for mystics if they cannot work on both levels: they give themselves up entirely to the nebulous, lunar dimensions of reality. Of course, in doing so they experience joy and even ecstasy, but their earthly tasks are left undone and even their bodies deteriorate from neglect. If you want to develop harmoniously it is essential to learn to function on both levels.

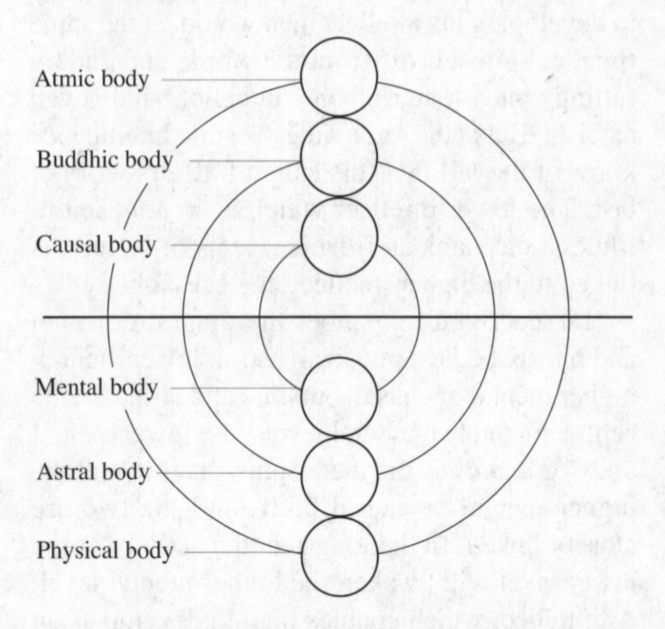

The sun prevents us from seeing the rest of creation which, nevertheless, is very real. In fact the universe contains many suns far bigger and more powerful than ours. But even if the light from our sun prevents us from seeing the rest of the universe, we must not hold that against it! It is a necessary, indispensable phenomenon and it corresponds to the work of the intellect. In the distant past, when men's intellects were not very developed, they did not have any vivid awareness of the physical world either. They lived and functioned primarily on the psychic and astral planes. They were in constant touch with the spirit world and projected themselves with ease onto the astral plane, voyaging in unseen regions and communicating with the dead. But later on Nature decided that human beings should develop their intellect, and now it has become so highly developed that intuition, clairvoyance and mysticism have been pushed into the background. There are, of course, a few who have maintained their contact with the subtler areas of reality, but most human beings have lost all contact because they function too exclusively on the intellectual level.

And yet, this intellect which, for the moment, has pushed the divine world out of sight, is capable of rising to far greater heights. The day will come when it will establish contact with the higher levels of intelligence to which it is linked: the pure, sublime intelligence of primary causes. When this day comes, men will know not only the objective, concrete, material world but also the subtle, invisible world. They will, once again, be in touch with the spiritual, the divine. We must never try to do without the intellect for, of all the faculties God has given us, it is the intellect that enables us to seek Him out. If we did not have this intelligence, however limited and mediocre it may be, we would never discover anything at all.

God gave men intellectual faculties so that they could use them to seek Him out and find Him, and with only a little goodwill this would not be so terribly difficult. Let me give you an example: when a murder or a robbery has been committed the police arrive on the scene of the crime to take fingerprints and look for clues. Why? Obviously because they know very well that there is necessarily an author behind every act. But then how is it that human beings do not seem to follow the same line of reasoning in respect to the existence of the universe? If they did, they would have to conclude that the universe, with its complex laws and the order and harmony that reign in it, must also have an author. Oh, no! Everything has an author except Nature. The oceans and mountains, the suns and constellations, all the living creatures of the universe have been brought into being by no one! What an utterly disastrous piece of reasoning.

We must take care not to underestimate the intellect. I have often talked about how it manifests itself nowadays and about the limits it should respect, but I have never had the intention of belittling its value or of denying that it has an extremely important role to play. It is thanks to the intellect, after all, that-we can learn to know the Lord, our Creator. But human beings really should try to be a little more logical: if, on the one hand, you admit that every crime must necessarily have an author and, on the other, you deny that the universe must also have its author, it is patently absurd. Human beings are so gullible about some things and so inconceivably incredulous and sceptical about others. They believe neither in a Creator nor in Cosmic Intelligence nor in the existence of a world hidden from our physical vision. They believe neither in justice nor in mercy and yet they are ready to believe that they should be able to reap great rewards without ever having planted a single seed. If they knew about reincarnation and the law of cause and effect they might realize that it is no good just waiting and hoping. You have to prepare the ground if you want to get what you ask for. They might realize that if they had worked harder in previous incarnations they would have all they want in their present lives.

It seems to me that human beings refuse to believe in Divine Intelligence, and yet they believe in the absurd and in blind chance. Some materialists even believe that atoms combine by pure chance to form brains endowed with intelligence. But just ask a farmer if his crops grow by chance: he knows very well that you cannot grow figs on a grapevine, nor plums on thistles. And if he knows that much he will also know that intelligence will produce intelligence and the absurd can produce only the absurd. How can scientists possibly believe that stupid, witless, chaotic chance can have created a world so intelligently organized? Really, it seems incredible!

III

The alternating rhythm of day and night teaches us that man must learn to live in two worlds: he must develop his intellect and acquire a clear perception of the physical world with all its details, but he must refuse to confine himself to the physical aspect of reality, otherwise he will never be a whole human being. Immensity, which is the realm of the heart and soul, will be lacking in him. A wise man knows that he must be in communion with all the souls of the universe without neglecting his work in the physical world. He lives both in the divine and the physical worlds and he therefore benefits from the advantages of both. To my mind if someone is a materialist it shows his lack of intelligence because he has obviously never studied things as they really are. He has put all his faith in his intellect and, since the intellect is the assassin of reality, true reality is never revealed to him.

Now, please do not misunderstand me: I have no intention of belittling the importance of the sun. Our sun is linked to the spiritual sun and is, therefore, our best means of communication with the spiritual sun. Similarly, our inner sun, our intellect, is linked to the sun on the causal level, which is universal wisdom and absolute knowledge. Our sun, therefore, is a stepping stone, a doorway. So do not let me hear you say, 'Oh, if the sun conceals reality from me I'll never go near him again!' He does not really hide reality, or rather, he hides it, only from those who are incapable of seeing beyond his visible, physical reality.

The light of day awakens us to the importance of this earth and of all its details: even little things are important. And yet the night reveals the unimportance, the insignificance of little things. When you are worried about something, when you have a problem on your mind, contemplate the stars in the night sky and gradually you will feel all your negative feelings slipping away from you. You will feel yourself becoming more magnanimous, more generous and indulgent. You will even find yourself laughing at some of the little things that had vexed or hurt you. As soon as he tears himself away from the petty reality of earth and takes off into immensity, man acquires nobility. He fuses into one with the Universal Spirit. And then, once more, he has to come back to earth and take up where he left off. For he cannot simply vanish into space, he has to get on with his work and fulfil his day-to-day obligations. If you have no time to contemplate the stars you can, at least, put yourself trustingly in the Lord's hands before going to sleep, saying, 'Lord, help me to know, understand and visit all the glories of Your Creation.' If you do this you will journey far during the night instead of stagnating on earth.

Man was not made to be earthbound but to travel to other planets and stars. The soul will meet no obstacles on its journeys through space. Of course our bodies are too condensed, they cannot take off and fly through space, but our souls know no barriers or obstacles. At the same time, however, if the soul is to travel free, its bonds with the body must not be too powerful. If physical appetites, lust and covetousness bind the soul too closely to the body it will not be able to soar free and taste higher joys.

Now suppose you are trying to meditate, but a heavy, cloudy sky is weighing you down and making it difficult, what should you do? Well, since the weather conditions are not conducive to mental activity, why not shift the emphasis from the conscious to the subconscious level? Let yourself float away on the cosmic ocean of love and delight. Give yourself over to God with a trusting heart, saying, 'Lord, allow me to be borne away on the ocean of light. I place all my trust in You.' Then you keep a tiny flame alight in the mind so that nothing evil can slip in and you let yourself go, floating on an ocean of joy and blessedness. This is a good way of dealing with days like that: just let yourself be cradled in peace, thinking of nothing, but without falling asleep, of course, and simply glancing into yourself from time to time to see what is going on.

The Sacred Books tell us that if we can suspend thought we can attain beatitude and immortality. But it is extremely difficult to suspend all thought and remain alert at the same time. To be in a state of complete silence in our minds, without falling asleep, without thinking, just feeling; it is very difficult. It is a state in which we feel and at the same time understand without knowing exactly how we understand or what instrument we use to reach that understanding. We only know that it is not our brain. The brain is not the only organ capable of understanding. Maybe physiologists have not yet discovered this, but I know and I can tell you that the brain is not the only instrument that has been specially prepared to understand; there are others.

If you compare the solar plexus and the brain you will see that although they are both made of the same grey and white tissue, they are differently organized: in the brain the grey matter is on the outside and the white matter on the inside, whereas in the solar plexus it is just the reverse. The function of the grey matter is to understand and that of the white matter to feel. The grey matter of the brain disposes us to understand the visible, exterior aspects of reality whereas the grey matter of the solar plexus disposes us to understand the inner, more secret, spiritual aspects of life.

Light and darkness are two divine principles. There is nothing evil in night any more than there is in day. Evil exists in men's minds and it comes from the fact that they do not understand everything. In Nature evil does not exist. Darkness and light both do the work they were intended to do, light flows from darkness, darkness produces light. In your spiritual work this is something you must never forget.

Chapter 3

SPRING WATER OR STAGNANT WATER

Have you ever listened to a tiny spring of water bubbling up from the ground? You should, bemuse it has a message for you. It is saying, 'Be like me. Come alive and give of yourself, otherwise you'll become a swamp!' It is very important to listen and take in this message bemuse if your own inner spring runs dry, things will begin to moulder and decay within you. And you know that when rot and mould set in they attract flies and vermin of all kinds. Once this happens, the vermin reproduce so fast that the only way to get rid of them is to dry out the swamp and clear away all the debris from the channel, because a free-flowing current of water washes away rot and vivifies and purifies its surroundings.

I have often talked about the importance of a spring, not only a little mountain stream, but the most powerful and abundant of all springs, the one and only fountainhead: the sun. If you see how people reason, however, and the attitudes they adopt it is all too obvious that they have never bothered to think about the symbolism of a spring, that central, vibrant source that flows and gives of itself without cease. The reaction of most people would be, 'What good can it possibly do to picture a spring in my mind?' Poor things! They may be very knowledgeable about many things but they have never understood the one thing that counts: that every one of their acts, in fact the whole of their existence, is guided and determined by the pictures they have in their minds. Do those pictures speak to them of life, of giving and outpouring like a spring or like the sun? Or are they images of death and decay like a swamp? Here you have the question in a nutshell. From my own observations I can say that everything depends on a person's choice, symbolically speaking, between the spring and the swamp. The choice he makes reveals his understanding, his outlook on life.

One often hears people complain that everything they do seems to turn sour. Why? Because the first priority in their minds and souls is not given to all that is pure and divine: the spring. If it were, the springwaters would flow and purify their inner landscape, causing the seeds of divine life within them to grow and prosper. Their mental attitudes and the things they set their hearts on show that they are not interested in what is essential : the one centre, one source, one sun, one spirit, one love. All their attention is concentrated on petty, insignificant details and they do not understand. They do not want to understand. They spend their time puddling around in stagnant, polluted waters and sneer at initiatic philosophy which constantly insists on the magical power of this link with the spring. Do they really believe that decay and mould, something that is rotting away, can be of any use to them?

Many people wonder why we go to see the sun rising in the morning. What we do is symbolic: we do it in order to reinforce in ourselves the realization that in every area of our, lives we must maintain our ties with the sun, the source. But have you ever tried to convince 'intelligent' people to go and watch the sun rising? It is utterly useless! They prefer what is dead, stagnant, polluted. And then, when things begin to go wrong, they wonder why? If they were not so blind it would be obvious to them that it is because there is so much impurity within themselves, because they do not follow the example of a spring.

Sometimes I ask, someone, 'Have you ever seen a natural spring? Can you tell me what it's like in the vicinity of a spring?' He may say, 'Of course I can!', but in point of fact I can see that he is not very observant, so I ask him something else, 'What can you find in the neighbourhood of a spring?' 'Plants. Vegetation.' 'What else?' 'Insects, birds, animals.' 'And what else?' 'Human beings come and settle there.' 'Right! But then, have you seen what happens when the spring dries up? Grass is the first to disappear, then animals, then human beings. Trees are the last to disappear. Have you understood all that?' 'Yes, of course. It's very simple.' 'Very well, but if it's so simple, how is it that you have allowed your own spring to dry up?' 'What spring? I don't understand! '

You see? He does not understand. He has never understood. People always think they understand, but it is only on the surface. So then I explain, 'The spring I'm talking about is inside you. Why have you let it dry up?' And he insists that he does not know what I am talking about, 'What spring? I've never let any spring dry up.' 'Oh yes, you have. You've let your own, inner spring run dry. There's no more love flowing from you. Perhaps, at some time, someone offended or injured you, or you were robbed and betrayed and you said to yourself, "That's the end. I'm never going to love or be generous and charitable again. People just don't deserve it." So now there is no more water flowing from you. Of course no one will ever betray you or break your heart again so you're under the impression that you've gained by your attitude. But in fact you've lost everything. You should have gone on being betrayed, if necessary, but you should never have let your spring dry up! You may well have been robbed, insulted and betrayed, but that's nothing compared to the blessing of having a free-flowing spring within you. That spring can give you everything you need. It can cleanse and renew everything.'

Human beings are desperately in need of this philosophy inspired by a spring. It is the most wonderful, the truest of all philosophies. Without it just look at what happens: because of some minor offence someone decides he has had enough of loving people, he will never fall into that trap again, with the result that he himself is finished: dead and done for! And what has he gained in the process? I never cease to be amazed at how human beings reason! And to think that some people believe I should learn from them. But I ask you: what would I learn? No! I would rather go on learning from a spring of water. I would rather stay beside it for hours, listening to its murmur, looking at it, touching it, speaking to it. And then I would be reminded of that other spring, the sun, and all the springs in the universe, until I reached the ultimate, the only true spring and source: God Himself. And I would try to create a link with this source that would help me, at last, to understand the essence of reality. So, if you ask me what I can understand from contemplating a spring, I have to say, 'Everything!'

Meditate at length on the symbolism of the spring so that your whole life may be founded on God, the one and only spring whose most perfect representative on earth is the sun. You should put this into practice every day. Take the sun, that inexhaustible spring, as your model and learn to give a draught of fresh water to all creatures, learn to give them warmth and light, to raise them from the dead. You will, perhaps, protest, 'But that's crazy! It can't be done.' If that is what you think it only goes to show that you have really not understood the first thing about it. It does not matter if your ideal is unattainable, an impossible dream. What matters is that by accepting to work towards it, it is you, yourself, who will be the first to benefit from it. The efforts you make in attempting to reach your goal will transform you like magic. The sun is immense, that is true. No human being can become as great and powerful as the sun, but in his own way and on his own scale, man can become a sun. Instead of eternally grabbing everything for himself, instead of acting like a gaping, hungry hole or a treacherous bog, instead of trailing death and destruction with him, wherever he goes, man can learn to give of himself, to have a cleansing, purifying influence and to communicate life. In point of fact, therefore, this ideal is not an impossible dream, it can be attained. But of course, one must at least *want* to study and learn and put certain things into practice, and to find out for oneself that it is possible.

Unfortunately, the more I see of life, the clearer it becomes to me that people do not understand the magical power of a spring. They simply do not realize how tremendously powerful it is nor how profound and mysterious a science it conceals. If they understood the lesson a spring holds for us they would always radiate something pure and vital from within. Instead of which they are constantly gloomy and lacklustre, unreceptive and tense. They never envisage any approach other than that of the swamp in attempting to solve their problems. But methods learned from a swamp never solve anything. On the contrary, they only prolong the lives of the tadpoles and other little creatures teeming in their stagnant waters.

As for the poor wretches who live permanently in a swamp, they are obliged to breathe and ingurgitate each others' waste. And, unfortunately, this is exactly the situation with human beings: big cities, in fact the world as a whole, is nothing more than a swamp. All the teeming millions of men and women on earth are obliged to absorb each others' excrement. Those who know how, take a gulp of purity from time to time, but the others let themselves be suffocated and poisoned. The atmosphere of a town is just like a swamp and if you were clairvoyant you would see how human beings shower each other with filth, how they devour each other. No one has any idea how to escape, if only for a few minutes. And to think that they only jeer at our solar philosophy! Well, so much the worse for them. Let them stagnate in their swamp if that is what they want. What else can I say? One day they will be forced to understand.

And now, what conclusion can we draw from what I have just been saying? It is this: all misunderstandings, all suffering and misfortune stem from the fact that human beings are not in contact with Heaven, the fountainhead. And even when they do, occasionally, establish contact with the Lord, it is cut off after only a few minutes and, once again, they drop back into their swamp. I do not want to offend you. Let's say that I am speaking 'in general'. But it is true, nevertheless. Instead of opening up a channel to the fountainhead that could purify, illumine and heal us, most people open a channel to a bog (which could equally be another human being or a group of people) and are content to drink its stagnant waters. They prefer their bog-water to the pure waters of a spring because they are afraid of the opinion of their fellow bogdwellers. What would the other tadpoles say? If ever the tadpoles ostracized them what would become of them!

You may be offended by what I say, but what can I do about it? I am not here for your amusement. I am here to tell you the truth. I know it is not very pleasant to listen to this kind of truth but if you are upset by what I am saying today, I must warn you that if I say nothing, one day you will be twice as upset, a hundred times more upset by reality. If you remain ignorant you will be an easy prey to the suffering and distress that are lying in wait for you on all sides, whereas if you are forewarned you have a chance of slipping out by the back door and your enemies will slink away with their tails between their legs!

So, think about these two contrasting images: the spring and the swamp. As soon as you want to love, as soon as you are ready to sacrifice something in order to help others and to give instead of taking, your spring has already begun to flow. And once this happens, flowers and trees will begin to grow, and the birds will begin to sing, which means that many beautiful, exalted spiritual entities will come and dwell in your mind, your heart and your will because they know that they will find nourishment there, the nourishment provided by the spring. When this happens it shows that you are like a rich, prosperous country with a large population and a flourishing civilization. And all this simply because the spring waters flow. This is how we should understand the symbolism of the spring.

You will never find anyone who is willing to live next to a spring that has dried up. When the springwaters cease to flow in a man there is no more creativity, no more poetry or music, no joy; nothing. Only wastelands and deserts, because there is no more water, no more love. All over the world one sees only deserts, millions of walking deserts! This is why people are in such a state of distress, nowadays, and feel such emptiness. They may be very intelligent but they have let their springs run dry because they have never thought of giving or loving or radiating life. When I see people whose waters have ceased to flow – or which have never flowed – I know that there is a sorry fate in store for them because nothing of beauty will ever dwell in them: neither angels, nor spirits of light, nor beauty, nor glory, nothing!

Blessed are they who have understood and decided to change! From now on everything will become crystal-clear to them, for these two concepts, the spring and the swamp, explain everything. If you are stagnant, if you have no enthusiasm for anything you do, if nothing brings you joy or inspiration, you now know that it is because the spring that should bubble up within you has run dry without your realizing it. This explains why you are always criticizing others. Leave the others alone and look after your own spring: open it up and clear away the rubbish, and water will begin to flow from it once again. It will have to flow, for we have been born to become springs. When God sent man to earth He prepared him to be a spring but man has accumulated so much filth in himself that the spring is blocked up and the result is a vacuum, a desert. And nothing is worse than a vacuum. Nothing is worse than finding yourself in a desert, than being a desert oneself.

Are you at last beginning to have some inkling of what the image of a spring means? A spring is life and love, and love is all-powerful. All inspiration, all joys are fruits of love. There is no greater truth than this. I know very well that in spite of all the truths you have been hearing for years, many of you are still in a sorry state because they have never learned to work methodically. Whatever I say to them, however many truths they hear which should help them, they never make a note of anything, so they forget it all immediately. If they wrote down just one truth and put it where they would he sure to see it every day, they would at least be in touch with it. But no! An hour after listening to a talk they have already forgotten everything they heard. People like that are predestined to stay indefinitely in their swamps or their desert. It is their own fault. Even when they are told what they should do for their own happiness they do not understand. They do not even remember what you tell them!

I know that I have often spoken to you about the spring before but you need to hear the same things repeated several times. The sun rose yesterday, but that was for yesterday. Today it has to rise again. Running water always looks the same but, in fact, it is constantly new. That is why I keep repeating, 'Make sure that your spring is open and that water is flowing from it every day. Remember to keep it open and pure and you will become a rich and fertile land and even kings will come and visit you to taste of the fruits growing in your garden.' I have been saying this for years and I still have to repeat it, time and time again. Why have you still not planted anything? Why have you never produced any crops in spite of all that rich and fertile land within you? For that is what your mind is: rich, fertile land. And you have an obligation to dig it, seed it and water it.

So, by means of your thoughts and prayers, open up the canals that will bring you water from the Heavenly Spring. We are all made in the image of God – the microcosm in the image of the macrocosm – so we too have a spring within us which is waiting for the right conditions before it will start to flow. And we can provide the conditions it needs by connecting up with the Spring on high. When we do this it will set our own spring flowing and all our cells will be watered and vivified by the flow of divine life. Thanks to that source which is love, life and living waters, we can become a perfect tool in the hands of God.

Chapter 4

MARRIAGE, A UNIVERSAL SYMBOL

I

We all know that love is the main topic of interest in most films, plays, novels, songs or poems. Love and marriage. The question of love and marriage needs no discussion: everyone knows that men and women are born with a need for love and, for the majority, with the need to bind themselves in marriage to their beloved. Of course it is true that love and marriage do not always go hand in hand. Sometimes love exists without marriage and sometimes there is marriage but no love. But generally speaking, a man and woman who love each other tend to marry and live together and try to stay faithful to each other. So we can say that it is normal for men and women to fall in love and get married. That is the way of the world.

So, we all agree: love and marriage are what you are most concerned about. And that being so,

I would like to ask you some questions and I wonder if you will be able to answer me. My questions are these, 'What do love and marriage mean to you? What do you understand by love and marriage? Why do you need to marry? Or rather, leaving aside the question of marriage, why do you think people feel the need to be in close contact with someone else, to unite themselves to another, to become one with another, if only for a few moments?' Who can give me the answer? Very few people seem to have asked themselves these questions, 'That's the way things are, why bother our heads about them?' Ah, but Initiates are in the habit of asking questions about every aspect of existence. They want to gain a deeper understanding of life and they have discovered that this human tendency, which is so natural and so universal, to seek out another human being and to unite with him, conceals one of the most significant secrets of the universe. If men understood the full significance of this tendency and knew how to make use of it in their spiritual work, they would fast become divinities.

Tradition has it that, in the beginning, human beings were created both male and female. Every man, therefore, is also a woman and every woman is both woman and man. To be a man or a woman is to be only half a human being and so each human must still find his or her other half. The trouble is that no one knows that we must look for our other half within ourselves. True marriage for every man and every woman is union with the other half of their being within themselves, not an exterior union with someone of the opposite sex. True marriage is to seek out and attract to oneself one's missing half, to melt into one with him or her and become, at last, a whole human being in order to accomplish works of magic.

Most human marriages on earth are only experiments, relatively successful or unsuccessful 'trial runs' while awaiting the day when it will be possible to achieve the spiritual reality of true marriage. In Indian religions true, spiritual marriage is symbolized by the Linga, an emblem representing the masculine principle as a vertical form combined with the horizontal Yoni, representing the feminine principle. The Linga is a reminder that the two principles must always be present in every human being. In the long run, every man and woman must achieve the unification of both principles within themselves. As you well know, this is extremely difficult. More often than not, when a man and a woman are physically united they are, in fact, separate and apart. But it is not physical apartness that matters. What does matter is that every individual should achieve, within himself, a true marrying of the two principles.

If you understand the mystery of marriage you will understand all the secrets of life. Marriage is the most widespread of all realities and yet very few people have any idea of its deeper meaning. Is a man bored? Let him try marriage as a cure for his boredom! Does he need sensual pleasure? Let him look for a partner to satisfy his need! Is he poor? Let him marry for money! He cannot look after himself? Let him find a good home-maker or let her look for a bread-winner! What human beings have made of the institution of marriage does not bear thinking of!

For me, marriage is something so sublime that I am not at all sure that I have really grasped what it means. What I am sure of is that it is only marriage, true, spiritual marriage that makes it possible to accomplish great things. A man may have great strength, the masculine quintessence, but as long as he is not married within himself he is incapable of condensing that quintessence into something visible, tangible and real on the physical plane. He lacks the feminine principle which alone can supply the matter necessary for physical manifestation. And if a woman is not married within herself, she may well have all the materials necessary, but she lacks the flame, the spark that can set them alight. She may possess a wealth of matter but if that matter is not ignited by the spirit it will remain stagnant and lifeless. This is something you must never forget.

II

Marriage is so vast a reality that we can learn something about it from every one of its myriad manifestations throughout Nature. Chemistry, physics, astronomy, botany, anatomy, physiology and so on, all speak to us of marriage. Take the case of water, for example, which is so indispensable to life in the universe. Water, H_2O, is a child born of the union of a father, oxygen, and a mother, hydrogen. And why is there only one atom of oxygen whereas there are two atoms of hydrogen ? Because one is the number which represents the masculine principle and two is the number of the feminine principle.

Or take the example of human speech: what do human beings use to produce words? Their arms and legs? Their ears? Their noses or their stomachs? None of these: they use their mouths and the mouth consists of a tongue and two lips.

When the tongue and the two lips interact they articulate a word. The tongue represents the masculine principle and the two lips the feminine principle. So the two parents, the two principles, produce a child: the word. You see what a marvellous lesson about reality is contained in this page of Nature's Book?

If philosophers had ever thought seriously about the mechanism involved in producing human speech they would have understood, by analogy, that God contains within Himself both the masculine and the feminine principles and it is by means of their interaction that He brought forth His Son, the Word, who in turn sets in motion the whole of creation. For the word is not meaningless or without purpose. On the contrary, it is addressed to someone for a definite reason. St. John tells us, 'In the beginning was the Word...' The word represents movement, the child.

Now we are getting to the heart of what I want you to understand. Just as God created the world by His Word so also, on the physical level on earth, human beings create life. In our mouths, the two principles are together, always united. In order to utter articulate speech the two lips and the tongue have to unite in producing sounds. Try to say something intelligible without moving your lips or your tongue: it cannot be done. In God the two principles are always present, together. They are never separated and that is why God creates ceaselessly. Whereas human beings behave as though the two principles were two distinct, independent realities, the masculine principle being the prerogative of men and the feminine principle the prerogative of women. And since the two must become one to create life, all kinds of difficulties and complications arise.

A living creature who fails to develop both the masculine and feminine principles within himself is not really in the image of God. He has not attained the fullness of being for which he was created. Of course, I am not talking about the physical expression of the two principles. I am talking about the spiritual reality: the principles of love and wisdom united and conjoined. Only those who have attained the unification of these two principles within themselves dwell in truth and possess genuine strength and power. And the only ones to have attained this level are the great Masters, the true Initiates, who have grasped the meaning of the Blessed Trinity of Love, Wisdom and Truth. These are God's true representatives on earth, power lines direct from God to us. It is they alone who dwell in fullness and they alone should be our models.

Speech can be creative and give form to matter only if it is charged with love and intelligence.

Empty, senseless words produce nothing. So, you see, we have to study and work hard if we want to be able to utter words capable of producing an effect throughout the whole of Creation, on all levels and in all worlds, visible and invisible. Words capable of moving angels, archangels and spirits and even the elements. Words of power and effectiveness must necessarily be pregnant with light and intelligence but they must also breathe warmth and love, the fullness of love. When both light and love are present, then words become truly powerful. I hope this is now clear to you. When you speak to your friends, to your husband or wife or to your children and your words fail to get the results you had hoped for, you will realize that it is simply because they are still not sufficiently warm and luminous.

Each one of us, all human beings possess symbols of cosmic importance in our mouths. Everyone has a mouth and, unfortunately, most people use it to complain instead of to express gratitude. Gratitude, in the first place, for being in possession not only of a mouth but of a tongue as well! We have to be careful not to make mischief with our tongues, however. You have probably heard the saying, 'The tongue has no bone in it but it can break bones.' If we are neither intelligent nor wise, neither reasonable nor kindhearted, we can break other people's bones with our tongues. We only have to wag our tongues and families are broken, people are massacred or condemned to death and we never raised a finger! We don't have to, we can do it all with our tongue.

It is high time we began to realize that when God gave us a mouth with a tongue in it, He gave us something of very great value. Yes, it is time to realize that and to use it to say, 'Dear Lord, forgive me. I'd never realized before what a treasure you had given me in putting a tongue in my mouth. I'd never realized that when I say a word I could imitate You, be like You, be a reflection of You. I'd never realized all that, and I've used words to do a great deal of damage. I've spoken a lot of empty, senseless words, I've wounded other people, I've upset a lot of creatures and played havoc with this instrument you gave me. Instead of using it to do good, to comfort others and ease their burdens, instead of guiding others and pointing out the right way, instead of giving and restoring life, instead of uplifting others and giving them an impetus to come closer to You, our Lord and Creator, I have defiled and destroyed them. Forgive me, Lord, and teach me to use my mouth and my tongue to do good, to guide and comfort others, not only to eat and drink and talk nonsense without ever understanding anything.'

The mouth is such an extraordinarily powerful organ that we should go in constant dread of misusing it. We have to be extremely careful to speak only edifying, instructive, life-giving words and never to let anything venomous escape our lips. Even if you have to appear to scold or chastise, your only motivation must be to enlighten and help others. If you follow this rule you will be preparing an indescribably glorious future for yourself for, as it says in the Gospels, 'By your words you will be acquitted and by your words you will be condemned.' In other words, your future will be good or bad, bright or dark, heavenly or hellish, depending on the words you utter during your existence on earth.

All this means that our words play such an important role in the preparation of our future that we should never cease to think and meditate about it, for the rest of our lives. We must become deeply conscious of the importance of words, and every time we open our mouths to speak, take care that we do so only for good.

But let me go even deeper, a great deal deeper, into the significance of this idea and show you how the universe is a coherent whole with rigorous laws of correspondence. The sun speaks. He speaks and his word is life. He speaks and his word is light, the light that shines on earth, on plants, animals and human beings. The invisible sun which acts on the visible sun produces light and that light produces heat. Now, let's suppose that the tongue corresponds to the father, the two lips to the mother and the word to the child, then we see that the father's gift to the mother is the gift of the word, the life-giving word. The law is the same: just as the invisible sun acts on the visible sun, the visible sun, in turn, acts on the earth to fertilize it. Just as a man fertilizes a woman, so the word fertilizes hearts and souls. It is the same law at work and we conclude that the speaker is the father, the one who listens is the mother and children are born of their union.

You may ask, 'Does this mean that men, too, can be mothers?' Yes, indeed it does. Someone who listens to another is like a woman. It is a question of switching one's polarity. When a woman talks to her husband she assumes masculine polarity and her husband, who listens, assumes feminine polarity. And children – feelings, emotions, thoughts, decisions and actions – are born of their union. So, as you can see, the same principle applies in diverse circumstances and in all regions, all domains. It is always, unfailingly, the same, identical law at work and you have to learn to juggle with it from one level to another.

From now on, therefore, try to broaden your vision of reality. If you stay forever in the same groove, if you refuse to modify your understanding of things, you will never grasp the fullness of life, for everything is related and interconnected. 'As above so below.' Many people who believe in the spiritual dimension repeat this maxim without really understanding it because they do not know exactly what is meant by the words 'above' and 'below'. It might help you to understand if we replace these words by others representing different concepts, creatures, existences or worlds. What other word could we put in place of 'below'? Well, we might put the sexual organs, or earth, or womankind or matter or even hell. And in place of 'above'? We could put the brain, the sky or the sun, man, the spirit. Hermes Trismegistus gave us this maxim but he did not interpret it for us. It is up to us to find out what it means.

But the most striking thing is that he added, 'In order to achieve the wonders – or the miracle – of one thing,' so that the whole maxim reads, 'That which is below is like to that which is above and that which is above is like to that which is below in order to achieve the wonders of one thing'. That which is below, therefore, collaborates with that which is above and together they produce 'one thing', the child. But what does that mean? What is that 'one thing'? Hermes Trismegistus never explained this either, but as you see, the tongue and the lips are two things which combine to achieve the wonders of one thing, and that one thing can be the Word. What we can be sure of is that, in order to produce this one thing, the two elements must be present: the masculine and the feminine principles, that which is above and that which is below. When a man and woman conceive a child, one of them is above and the other below. The one who is below is like the one who is above: the difference is in the position. And the purpose is to achieve the miracle of one thing: a child.

So now I will leave you to think about all this. Try not to go through life blindly, uncomprehendingly, somnolent, unconscious. Make up your minds to live according to reason: give up everything that is holding you down, prisoners in the lower regions: all those sensations and trivial, useless occupations! Make up your minds to hold on only to essentials, and get down to work!

III

'That which is below is like to that which is above.' This maxim of Hermes Trismegistus reveals that marriage already existed above before it ever existed on earth. Above, in the higher realms of existence, the two cosmic principles, masculine and feminine, are forever united in a relationship of exchange, and human marriage on the physical level is a reflection of this union. This is. what Initiatic Science teaches. And in the Book of Genesis it says, 'In the beginning God created Heaven and earth.' Heaven and earth are symbols which we have to interpret, just as we have to interpret the relationship between them. Heaven and earth symbolize the two eternal principles: emissive and receptive, masculine and feminine. These two principles come together and children are born of their union. Everything in the visible world and even what is invisible to us has been brought into being by this union of the two principles. Everything on earth is the child, the offspring, of the union of Heaven and earth. If the earth were to break the bond, if it were no longer united to Heaven, Heaven would be unable to nourish it with its impetus and higher energies and the earth would become a desert.

Heaven and earth, the masculine and feminine principles, already exist on the highest, most sublime level of reality and are reflected onto the lower levels of reality, all the way down to the physical level. Everywhere and on all levels these two principles can be seen at work and their union produces forces and energies. When you want to plug an electrical appliance into the main power line you use male and female plugs. But have you ever noticed that they are both polarized? Two and two, every object, every being contains in itself the two poles. Heaven and earth, man and woman, each has two poles. So when contact is made, that makes four, and life-forces circulate and children are brought into the world. But without contact or union, without fusion and exchange between the two, nothing can happen.

Now, if we extrapolate onto the level of the inner, spiritual life we can see that as long as a human being is not in touch, in contact with the higher levels of reality, he will remain isolated and alone. And a human being who remains alone is barren and unproductive and sooner or later he will disappear without a trace. Perhaps you will object, 'But I have a wife (or a husband) and a whole brood of children!' That may be so on the physical level, but it is not enough. True marriage implies knowing how to work with the two principles on all levels. If you do what has to be done on the physical level, you will have results: children. There is no doubt about that! But this will not prevent you from being barren on other levels if you have never understood that the law of marriage must be applied on all levels, physical, astral, mental and so on.

'That which is below is like to that which is above and that which is above is like to that which is below.' 'Above' is the spiritual, divine region; 'below' is the physical world. Everything which exists on the physical plane corresponds to a higher reality on the spiritual plane. And on both levels it is of vital importance to be 'plugged in' to the mains. The Initiates concealed this truth in the symbol of the serpent swallowing its own tail: the symbol of true marriage. This may come as a surprise to you, 'How can a serpent swallowing its own tail be a symbol of marriage?' But it is not so far-fetched as it may seem at first sight. True marriage for human beings is exactly that: the union of the head and the tail. The other kind of marriage is only a reflection of this.

Man is divided, separated from himself in his consciousness and he needs to find that part of himself that he does not yet know and unite with it again. This is the idea behind the precept, 'Know thyself' which was carved over the entrance to the temple of Delphi. Very few people have ever understood that inscription. I once heard a lengthy explanation by a professor of the University of Paris and I was astounded at his ignorance. Even the most learned scholars have no inkling as to its true meaning. Their explanations have no depth or truth in them.

To know oneself does not mean to know one's character with all its faults and failings, nor to know the limitations of human nature. If it went no further than that even children could understand and know themselves. In this phrase, 'Know thyself', what is the 'self'? Our limbs? Our brains? Our thoughts and feelings? No, it is none of that. The Self we must know is a part of God, a spark, an immortal spirit, something indescribable but real which exists on a far higher level. To find and unite with this Self, human beings must reach up to greater heights. They will know themselves only when they know that indestructible, omniscient, all-powerful being, the higher Self which is a tiny part of God Himself. At this level man realizes that he depends on God for his existence, that he is united with God and has no separate or independent existence or activity. When he has truly grasped this he sees, too, that everything he has ever felt or thought was illusory and unreal. The only reality is that inner, higher Self, who is God. If he does everything in his power to anchor himself in God, to be aware always that he is a part of God, one with Him, then his consciousness melts into the Eternal One and he can draw on the reservoirs of His power, light and love. He no longer feels as though he were tiny and apart, alone and abandoned to suffering. He feels himself to be God.

I have already explained this to you at length: as long as you identify with your physical body you will be weak, vulnerable, subject to death like the physical body, and affected by every slightest thing that happens to it. But if you cease to see yourself simply as a physical entity swayed by instinctive impulses, and identify yourself instead with the Centre of the universe, the Source of life, the Creator, then you will gradually distance yourself from weakness, decrepitude, sickness and death and move towards oneness with the everlasting, all-knowing and all-encompassing Godhead. This is why Initiates of old were so insistent that man should know his real Self. As long as human beings are content to know everything except their own selves, they will never reach the goal to which, after all, every single one of us aspires: freedom, peace and happiness. To know oneself means to melt into the immensity of God.

I hope this is quite clear to you now: when the Initiates of Ancient Greece said, 'Know thyself' they were in no way recommending that we should recognize our faults and failings, because our vices, faults and failings are not our Self. You must get this absolutely clear in your minds.

Of course, it goes without saying that it is not possible to become one with God overnight! Many people, even in a lifetime, will never reach this higher level of consciousness or feel their oneness with the Eternal Being. From time to time, perhaps, they will see a glimmer or have a fleeting illumination, but the very next day they will once again feel isolated, powerless and dejected. Whereas someone who has reached oneness with his higher Self is in a permanent state of peace and light. He feels himself to be immortal. His consciousness reaches so high and so wide that he perceives all other beings as part of himself. He has no enemies and he loves every living creature because he senses that it is he himself who lives in every creature. He obeys the dictates of a higher moral law. 'Know thyself', therefore, means all this, too.

Not only does it take time to attain this degree of awareness but it also takes great inner discipline. In India this is known as Jnani-Yoga, and to help themselves reach this consciousness of their identification with God, Hindu yogis use the formula, 'I am That.' After years of meditating on these words, a yogi reaches a state of awareness in which he knows that he does not exist, that his Self is none other than 'That', the Lord God, the unique, all-powerful Being, the only Reality.

And now, what does it mean to 'know'? In the Bible we read that Adam, 'knew Eve his wife; and she conceived and bore Cain'. Does this mean that Adam did not know Eve before? Abraham, too, 'knew' his wife, Sara, and Isaac was born. Knowing, therefore, implies contact, the contact between two poles seeking to unite or, if you prefer, to 'taste' each other. Look at how small children react when they see something that intrigues them: they are curious, they want to discover what it is, to know it, so they put it into their mouths. They taste everything, because at that age it is the mouth and not the brain which is their organ for knowing, for making contact with physical reality. And you, yourself, what do you do when you want to experience a new scent or sound, or to become familiar with an object or an idea? You let it enter into you through your sense organs: your nose, ears, eyes, or through your mind. In other words, in order to know something we have to let it in, to let it penetrate us. And when it comes to bringing children into the world the same law applies. Knowing is achieved by penetration: something penetrates or enters into us and becomes a part of us.

Now, becoming one with an object or another living being supposes that our vibrations harmonize with theirs: we have to be tuned to the same wavelength. You can see this law at work if you have two tuning forks: you set one of them vibrating and if the other one is identical it will start vibrating also. It responds because it is tuned to the same wavelength. Therefore to know oneself, that is, to know the divine Being who dwells in us, we have to tune ourselves to the same wavelength and vibrate to the same rhythm. Without this attunement we can never truly 'know'.

Let me go back for a moment to the symbol of a serpent swallowing its own tail. The head which swallows the tail means that the masculine and feminine principles unite in order to attain self-knowledge. But suppose, for instance, that the serpent is very long, ten miles long, and one day as he is sliding along over the ground he meets a tail and out of curiosity he bites it! Only then does he realize that the tail is his own! Or watch how a kitten plays with its tail: if he happens to bite it he soon finds out that it is part of himself. The reality of a human being reaches far beyond his physical body. What we see here, on earth, is only our tail end. Our head is somewhere else, far, far away. And as long as our two poles, head and tail, are divorced from each other, we shall continue to be content to slither over the ground like snakes.

The tail has to seek out the head and unite with it. The tail is the lower self and it has to seek out and find the head, the higher Self, which dwells in the heavens, far above us. As soon as there is contact, interaction between the two, a steady flow of harmonious energies is released. In the human body the serpent is at the base of the spine. It is Kundalini. And Kundalini, once aroused, rises upwards the length of the spine. When the two poles are at last united, that is when Kundalini, 'below', is united with Siva, the universal Spirit 'above', and then man truly knows himself. He has attained the fullness of being.

'Know thyself.' The Self is not the tail threshing about on the physical plane below. It is the head, the spirit which is above. True marriage is true knowing. But man has not yet reached this stage. He 'marries' with all kinds of people and things exterior to himself He 'plugs in' and makes contacts in factories and offices, in politics and economics: everywhere except in his own inner Self. He does not know how to make contact with his inner Self and that is why he feels perpetually unfulfilled, unsatisfied.

Man's highest achievement is to merge his lower self with his higher Self, the tail with the head. Of course, I do not deny that the tail has some good points: it is capable of movement, for instance. But the head has so many more: it has eyes, ears, a mouth, a nose and even a brain. So, if we manage to become one with our higher Self we shall know everything it knows, see all that it sees, hear all that it hears; we shall have reached perfection. But as long as we remain divorced and separate, as long as we identify only with the tail, we shall be deprived of all that wealth.

The tail must join up with the head. We have to learn to 'make both ends meet.' Centuries ago the Initiates coined this phrase, but men have forgotten what it means. Nowadays they use it when they have financial problems: money is tight at the end of the month and they say, 'I can't make ends meet.' In reality the 'ends' in question are the head and the tail of the serpent. The true meaning of making ends meet is the development of the chakras, one after the other, beginning with Muladhara at the base of the spine, all the way to Sahasrara at the top of the head, in order to create unity. As long as we fail to 'make ends meet' we shall be condemned to poverty and privations and this is true on both the spiritual and the material level.

The fullness of creative power is found in marriage. Have you ever come across a man or a woman who alone was capable of bringing a child into the world? No, there always has to be two.

And this explains why someone who is not united with Heaven will always be a childless bachelor, or an old maid! You must get married! But you must get married to Heaven so as to produce a lot of offspring. The Book of Genesis says that God told man to, 'Be fruitful and multiply,' and men have always understood this solely on the physical level. Every commandment applies on at least three levels and can be interpreted, therefore, in three ways. But human beings are content with the lowest, physical interpretation and this is where they go wrong: they do not try to understand the higher meaning. We must be fruitful and multiply: true, but on the level of our thoughts and feelings and in order to produce a multitude of tiny, luminous, winged creatures who will influence the whole world and bring about the Kingdom of God on earth!

Oh yes! We have to think often and at length about marriage, but marriage on the highest level. This is the new understanding, the new philosophy.

The reason we go and see the sun rising every morning is that the sun is a centre, the centre of our solar system, and contemplating it helps us to centre ourselves. Our Selves, our true Selves, are not here on this earthly level. They dwell at a great distance from our bodies, in the sun. But they have a bond with our illusory little selves on earth, and each time we manage, consciously, to establish communications between the two, our lesser self is drawn up into the sun, where it experiences light and joy. That is why, if you remember, 1 have given you various exercises you can practise at sunrise. For instance, you can imagine that you are in the sun and from that vantage point you look down and smile at yourself on earth and say, 'Poor fellow! If you only knew how much better off you'd be up here!' In this way you are creating a bond between your lower self and your higher Self which will help you find your true identity. If you practise this exercise for years you will end by possessing all the qualities and virtues of your higher Self. Your true Self is immortal and knows everything that has ever happened on earth and he can tell you about it. He is absolutely free and can invest you with all powers. He lives in a boundless ocean of bliss and he can give you indescribable happiness.

When a man and a woman unite, they experience tremendous joy, but they do not know what it means. The joy experienced in a loving union goes to prove how truly important it is to 'make ends meet'. When a human being has achieved this goal he has achieved the fullness of his being, and the same joy and delight flood his soul. But the joy he knows at this stage is far subtler than that other. It is the joy of ecstasy that saints, yogis and Initiates achieve when they have found themselves.

So, there, in a few words, you have the secret of marriage. Every single one of you must marry but not only outwardly, for exterior marriage robs us of our strength. If we marry our inner, higher Selves, our strength increases and multiplies.

Chapter 5

DISTILLING THE QUINTESSENCE

Today I want to talk to you about the work you can do on the mental plane, using your power of thought. I know that a great many people have completely lost the habit of all mental activity: they never attempt to concentrate or meditate. They think it is pointless. Why waste precious time which could be used to do much more important things? People have become so used to acting only on the outer surface of reality that it is difficult to get them to envisage anything else. They have no idea that the work of the mind contains untold possibilities that no other activity can achieve.

Let's take an example: when you extract copper or iron ore from a mine you have to get tons and tons of ore before you can produce even a small quantity of pure metal. All the rest is the gangue or rock which is worthless. Similarly, if you want a few litres of Bulgarian essence of roses you will need several wagon-loads of rose-petals. But once you have extracted the essence it is worth a fortune. Generally speaking, most human activity is the equivalent of displacing masses of soil and rock, whereas the work of the mind makes it possible to extract the essence from the mass. If you never learn to use your minds to concentrate, to control and master yourself, to direct your energies and use them for a higher purpose, whatever else you do will be like accumulating mountains of raw materials which will simply be a burden to you unless you can extract the essence from it.

The prodigious amount of work accomplished by an Initiate is all done with a view to extracting the quintessence from brute matter. Quintessence is something intangible without which everything would be insipid and meaningless. Even if you possess all the wealth in the world, if you do not possess the quintessence which exists on the mental plane, you would still feel a void, you would still feel dissatisfied and restless. It is not quantity that gives meaning to life but quality, quintessence. Unfortunately, human activities are the symbolic equivalent of grinding up and storing huge quantities of stone and mineral ore without ever extracting the quintessence, because to extract the quintessence requires a totally different type of activity.

People spend their time working to earn money and yet, whatever they do, they are always dissatisfied. They complain that something is lacking. What is lacking is exactly that: the quintessence, that intangible, imponderable something that gives meaning to life. Human beings habitually think in terms of quantity whereas quintessence implies quality. Nowadays people are interested only in producing and consuming more and more. Quality does not interest them. But quantity designates the physical, material world, the earth, whereas quality designates the spiritual, divine level of reality.

It is only in an Initiatic School that one can learn to distil the quintessence of reality. An Initiatic School is like a distillery in which disciples learn to extract the essence from their total life experience. All they have accumulated in the form of thoughts, feelings and sensations, all their successes and failures, all their sufferings are put into the still and their quintessence, that is the lessons they contain, are extracted. The pure liqueur of wisdom and understanding flowing from the still enables the disciple to see the full purport of the laws at work in the different events and circumstances of his life and to understand why success crowned certain of his undertakings and others were failures.

An Initiate is a human being who possesses the quintessence of his own life. It is only a tiny phial but it is an inexhaustible reservoir of perfume. When an Initiate takes possession of the quintessence of his existence, of his being, he has found the purest and most precious thing there is: the quintessence of Creation which is God Himself. A quintessence is all that is most perfect in the whole of Creation. Only one tiny gramme of this precious substance emanates millions of particles and never diminishes. Man's quintessence is his spirit.

Modem scientists are enthralled by all they discover in the world around them but they never seem to be enthralled by their own selves. If they only knew; they themselves are a quintessence infinitely more precious than uranium or plutonium! It is mankind, we ourselves, who should be our principal source of wonder and astonishment, for it is man who is the most precious element. For billions of years, now, we have been radiating and we shall go on radiating for thousands of years more. It is a pity that people are always attracted by what is outside themselves. They are like children, unconscious of their own reality and very busy exploring their surroundings.

Since thought is the only means available to man by which to bring direction and harmony into his life, if he gives up all attempt to think and reflect he will slowly but surely sink down to Hell because Hell, too, is present in every man. Within each one of us Heaven and Hell both exist and we are free to choose the direction we want to take. More often than not a man chooses the path of disorder and chaos which leads straight to Hell, because he wants to be free and independent and to 'live his own life'. But do not let yourselves be fooled by ignorant people who try to persuade you to abandon all your spiritual aspirations. It is totally impossible to find happiness that way. Instead, listen to the Initiates who advise you to pray and meditate every single day. Of course, you cannot stop working in the world, you have your job and you have to go on earning your living. But still, you must never entirely give up the only thing that can lead to a richer, more intelligent life.

I am constantly struck by the fact that people work against their own best interest. They have done away with the one essential, the activity of the mind, that could give them the knowledge and mastery they need to live a life of glory. You have to begin working in this direction when you are young and it takes a great deal of patience and tenacity, but it is the only way to get good results.

When you excavate a mine in the bowels of the earth, you bring up tons and tons of earth and rock. That is the easy part. The difficult part comes when you want to extract a precious metal from all that rock. Mental work, too, is difficult. Most people imagine that meditation should show immediate results and when it fails to do so, they give up trying. Why be in such a hurry? It takes time to extract the most precious elements, a great deal of time. Try to understand what I am telling you: once you have begun this work you must never give it up. Devote at least a few minutes to meditating every day. An hour or two would be even better if you can. In fact, it would be better still to devote whole days to meditation if this were possible. A few minutes is very little. What quintessence can possibly be extracted in only a few minutes?

Look at all the impoverished, arid countries of the world in which fantastic underground wealth has been found: oil, natural gas, gold or diamonds. Similarly, however impoverished and down on his luck a man may be, if he understands these truths and begins to undertake a process of elimination and distillation in his life, his failures and misfortunes and errors will begin to yield their quintessence: wisdom and understanding. He will learn how the laws operate, discover the plans Providence has in store for him and begin to discern the path that lies ahead.

And, believe me, if you can distil the quintessence from your life you will become immensely valuable, like an undeveloped country which discovers diamonds in its subsoil and suddenly becomes immensely rich, thanks to these precious stones. Even if you are the poorest and most despised of men, you can become a multimillionaire and king of some precious virtue, quality or wisdom.

Thought is the most effective means we have of living the divine life, but on one obvious condition: that we concentrate our thought exclusively on the highest, best things. For everyone thinks. The question is *how* do they think? Have you ever seen someone stirring up a manure heap with his pitchfork? The most nauseating stench spreads far and wide. Well, this is how a lot of human beings think: they stir up the manure inside themselves and poison the atmosphere all around! Everybody thinks; there is not a living human being who does not think. Even when you are not concentrating on anything in particular you are still thinking. The trouble is that people think in the wrong way. So I am not saying that people should make the effort to think: they do so already. Thought existed before anything else and it takes precedence over everything else. Even the laziest people think, but their thought floats like leaves on the wind, while others think how to swindle and thieve and murder. Their minds are functioning, that is true. But that is not what I am talking about when I say that you have to learn to think.

In order to think correctly you have to know what to think about and how to do so. When I speak of our capacity for thought I am speaking about a tool, an instrument we possess and which we must use to bring us closer to the divine world: a world where light, certainty and peace reign. If our thinking does not bring us closer to that divine world it will, inevitably, bring us closer to Hell. In fact, the faculty of thought has equally strong ties with both worlds, so a lot of hard work is required to detach it from the infernal powers seeking to dominate it, and direct it Heavenwards. If you do not do this you will assuredly live in Hell and although you may be invited to sumptuous receptions where the great of this world gather to congratulate and flatter you, in reality you are in Hell. Whereas if you know how to direct your thought towards the divine world, even if you are all alone in a corner you will experience overwhelming joy, for you possess Heaven and earth within you. They belong to you. Of course, those who see that you are happy in the midst of privations may think, 'Poor fool! He's got nothing to be happy about.' But what does it matter what other people say?

Man is put together in such a way that he can vibrate in unison with both Heaven and Hell. The Lord has not restricted his movements. When people say, 'If God does exist He should prevent people from committing crimes.' I reply that to say that only shows how ignorant they are: God's greatness is revealed in the fact that He has given human beings the freedom to do wrong if they want to. If He had made it impossible for us to stray from the right way we should be robots. How could we manifest the glory of God if we were not free? We would all be obliged to sing the same tune and wouldn't that be dull! God must have said to Himself, 'It's going to be dreadfully boring if they all do exactly the same thing all the time. Let's give them some freedom.' And so now He is the spectator of the show... for, 'All the world's a stage'...

Oh, I know what you are going to say: you are going to say, 'You're contradicting yourself. You've already said, several times, that God never even looks to see what human beings are up to.' No, of course He never looks. Why should He? He knows exactly what men are capable of. Nothing can surprise Him because He knows in advance what is going to happen. So He has packed His bags and gone off to faraway heights where He is busy with other things and He leaves human beings to their own devices.

Well, it is not the moment to go into that. Today, what I am really interested in is getting you to understand the importance of never letting a day go by without concentrating, if only briefly, on a lofty, exalted idea, for in doing so you trigger forces of a higher order and establish contact with regions of the most sublime purity from which you can obtain help and support. Perhaps you will question whether the advantages of this practice are really as great as I paint them. Yes, indeed they are. They are immense. In the first place your health will begin to improve because you will no longer waste so much energy on interior and exterior battles. Also, you will begin to cleanse yourself of impure elements and enrich yourself with new, more spiritual elements. And finally you will begin to attract the attention and friendship of those subtle entities who dwell on higher planes. They cannot help but notice the beams of light you send out to pierce the darkness covering the earth and they feel obliged to take an interest in you.

So, get into the habit of meditating. It is extremely important. Of course, I am not advising you to live like yogis, meditating all day long. But nor do I recommend that you cut your ties with Heaven simply because you are busy and have to earn your living. The advice I am giving you is the very best: go ahead, make money, acquire knowledge and anything else you want, but also set aside some time in order to extract the quintessence from all your activities. If you do not do that, even if you make all the money in the world, if you never grasp the quintessence of your life you will always be unhappy. You will always have that feeling, lurking in the back of your mind, that all your belongings are pointless, a burden to you. Without that quintessence it will do you no good whatever to conquer the entire world.

And remember: that quintessence can only be obtained through your mental activity. When you come up against some great difficulty in your life, when you feel dejected and have lost all your material possessions, you still have the power of thought. So set it to work, concentrate your thought and direct it Heavenwards to make contact with higher entities and you will, unfailingly, feel that things begin to take a turn for the better. Through prayer and meditation you can regain everything you had lost. I have known people who have been so unhappy that they were on the brink of suicide, but then they prayed and prayed and made contact, mentally, with realms of such wondrous beauty that they realized they had not really lost anything. No one had done them any real wrong. And, once again, they felt themselves to be rich and happy within. This is what it means to possess the quintessence.

Chapter 6

THE POWER OF FIRE

Everyone has his own ways and, as you realize, I am no exception. You have so often heard me repeat the words, 'That which is below is like that which is above...' or the expression, 'The Great Living Book of Nature'. But at least my ways are useful, and I can prove it by showing you, once again, that this maxim of Hermes Trismegistus is a key which unlocks many a door for me.

I remember that when I was young, I must have been about thirteen or fourteen, I liked to try my hand at all kinds of trades. None of them lasted very long, of course, a few days or a few weeks at most. It was the holidays, school was over for the summer and instead of going to play with other children I preferred to get a job and learn a trade. And that is how I became a tailor! Oh, not for long. Only a day, in fact, because I must admit that I did not at all enjoy tailoring: I kept going to sleep! The only really good thing about being a tailor is the position. You know: tailor-fashion, legs crossed as in the Lotus position of Indian yogis. But even that did not prevent me from going to sleep because, well, sewing is not terribly exciting, is it? It seemed endless and then, too, I kept pricking my fingers. So I decided to give it up at the end of a day.

But still, you know, a day spent as a tailor leaves its mark and ever since I have always continued to sew, in my own way, without anyone noticing. I have never opened a boutique to make money that way, but I still continue to make my own clothes. Ah, you are surprised, aren't you ? Yes, I go to certain shops I know, choose the very best cloth and make myself beautiful clothes, the most gorgeous tunics and coats that have ever been made. I let someone else make my exterior garments for me, or I buy them ready-made, but for my interior garments: that is my job. I find that I am the only person capable of choosing them and making them fit. So, you see, I am my own tailor. And now I shall leave you to interpret this for yourselves.

But there was one trade above all which left an indelible impression on me. When I went for a walk I would often pass the blacksmith's shop, and I was so fascinated by the way the blacksmith would beat a piece of white-hot iron into shape, that I wanted to work with him. I stayed there several weeks and enjoyed it enormously, except that I only had sandals on my feet, so I kept getting sparks on them and they were covered with blisters. But I shall never forget the experience of that apprenticeship: it was my job to work the bellows and while I pumped I watched the blacksmith work. I can still remember how the sparks flew. It was magnificent!

And now I want to draw a lesson from this experience as a blacksmith to show you how I use the key of analogy. Everyone knows that if you want to forge iron you have to put it in the fire and wait for it to get red-hot and then incandescent, but very few ever stop to try and decipher the important initiatic secret hidden in this phenomenon. And yet it is one of the most significant pages of the living Book of Nature. How can a flame communicate its heat and even its light to a piece of iron? It is a mystery. The iron becomes exactly like the fire: luminous, radiant and burning hot. To begin with it is cold, dull, lifeless and relentlessly hard, and then it allows itself to be transformed and takes on new properties.

And human beings can be compared to a piece of metal, iron for instance: only the contact with fire can make them radiant, bright and warm.

Obviously I am talking about spiritual, not physical fire. There are different kinds of fire but only mystics really have any idea of the contact with spiritual fire: it is ardour, love, ecstasy, like an intense form of life. Yes, spiritual fire is a life capable of consuming and transforming you so that you become a different being. Just like physical fire which makes iron sufficiently pliant and tractable for it to be shaped into new forms, celestial fire, which is divine love, plunges man into a spiritual state in which he sloughs off his former hard, ugly, opaque form and acquires a radiantly bright new one.

This secret has always been known by true mystics and prophets, by Initiates. They know how to find the true fire which is the fire of the soul and the spirit. They know how to plunge themselves into it until they become so perfectly malleable that they can hammer themselves into new shapes. And they know, too, how to temper the newly shaped metal so that it will retain its form. Here again is a detail which very few interpret correctly: once a piece of metal has reached white heat it must be plunged into cold water so that its new form becomes hard and durable, and this is true on the spiritual level also. The cold water is represented by all the trials and sufferings that come our way. Fire melts metals and water hardens them whereas it is just the opposite for the earth: water makes the soil looser and more malleable and heat dries it out and hardens it. This is just one more aspect of the language of living Nature.

There are several different kinds of fire but they can all be put into one of three categories: physical, visible fire which consumes and devours material things; astral fire which torments human beings and which includes for instance, the fire of passionate, sexual human love; and the third category which is divine: divine fire, the fire of the sun which does not consume or cause suffering but which, on the contrary, brings us light, joy and rapture and the sublime sensation of being touched by God Himself. This is the fire of Heaven. But the fire most humans know best is the burning fire of their passions, and when they cry out that they are afire, consumed by flames, it is very often no more than a passing flame. What is so strange is that although the fires of passion cause them suffering and distress – they even start to lose weight – yet they still love it and keep falling into it! Very few know how to move onto a higher level and plunge into that sublime fire that fills the higher realms. But that is the fire which is most familiar to me. More than once in my life God has granted me instants in which I have truly tasted this heavenly fire.

If we want to transform ourselves and remodel our temperaments, our tendencies and habits, even our hereditary traits, we have to invoke fire from Heaven, attract it to ourselves and keep fanning the flame until we find ourselves melting. When we are as molten metal, then we can call on other beings to reshape us or, if we are sufficiently conscious, we can refashion ourselves. And now you see how I interpret the blacksmith's trade?

I have no hesitation in telling you how to transform yourselves because I have tested it for myself and I know it is absolutely true. Just as a smith works his bellows until the coals are white-hot, you must make use of prayer to implore the gift of divine fire, and when it comes it brings such heavenly effervescence to your inmost being that you cannot help but melt. It is impossible to have such an experience and not change inwardly and even outwardly; you will find that your physical appearance begins to change and you will fashion a new visage for yourself.

Yes, I have verified everything I tell you through personal experience. I have had the privilege and joy of experiencing, of tasting that celestial fire and it was then that I realized that it was capable of melting and refashioning old, time-honoured forms. That is why you should wish for nothing but this heavenly fire, think of nothing but this fire, contemplate it constantly until it sets you alight and transforms your heart and your whole being. Do not rely on explanations from others or on books: they can do nothing for you if your whole being does not vibrate and throb with the fire within, if you are not ablaze with fire, like the sun. For the sun is fire and that is why we should be there, every day, to see it rise and to renew our contact with the fire from Heaven. If you tune in to the sun, if, wholeheartedly and with all the powers of your intelligence, you let the sun set you ablaze, flames will rise from you and enfold you. The Holy Spirit is none other than the sacred fire of the sun.

Put your trust in the sun. Only he can infuse this fire into you. Only the sun can set you on fire and make you burn and glow. Never let a day go by without a moment of conscious communication with the sun until the divine fire dwells in you and reveals all things to you. This is the kernel of every initiation: whatever you get out of life will be as nothing without this fire. So reach out to this fire and do not be afraid of being burned: it does not burn, it transforms. Or, if you like, you can say it burns, but it only burns away waste and impurities, it does not destroy what is pure, noble and divine. Fire cannot harm another fire. it cannot destroy what is of the same nature as itself.

If you read Ezekiel, St. John or any of the other prophets you will see that they all tell of how God purified their lips with a burning coal or made them swallow a little scroll. The outward manifestations vary but the inner reality is the same: from the air, through our breathing, a spirit enters into us. Call it the Holy Spirit, if you like. Hindus say it is a kind of prana from Heaven, others say it is fire, or light. It does not much matter what you call it, it is a spirit which is given to us, which we breathe in from the air. This is why some Initiatic philosophies attach such importance to breathing or respiration: inspiration and expiration, the beginning and the end, God Himself, eternal life. Life begins with the first breath, the first inspiration, and when someone dies we say he 'expires'. It is important to be attentive to this question of respiration and understand its full significance.

At meals, for instance, are you in the habit of breathing correctly? People bring illness on themselves because instead of breathing properly while they eat, they talk and gesticulate and gulp down their food. At first sight breathing may seem to bear no relation to eating, but in fact, it is impossible to nourish oneself properly if one's breathing is not harmonious. Nobody has ever taken the subject seriously but it is very important not to talk while you eat and to breathe correctly, for if you breathe correctly you absorb not only the solid, material elements in the food, but also the subtler elements and, in this way, you build up reserves for the whole day. So, although it may not seem especially useful to pause for a few deep breaths during a meal, in fact this practice speaks of important, hidden truths. But people are a long way from all this! So I advise those of you who are new to our Teaching not to be astonished and not to criticize or compare our methods with the instruction you received in the world. You must be patient and study this Teaching with perseverance and, one day, you will marvel at the light that dawns in you when you realize what wealth our Teaching and our methods really contain. At first sight they may seem trivial but, in fact, they open the way for something entirely new and different from everything you have known up to now.

You must have realized by now that my philosophy has not come from reading books, but from my own experience. I never reveal something to you which I have not put into practice for a long time. And even now, I am always experimenting, getting to know and putting into practice other truths in the hope of passing them on to you one day. So, trust me and make up your minds, here and now, that you are going to know and feel the power of celestial fire within yourself, that you are going to possess it. And in order to achieve this, concentrate intently, far more intently, on the sun and the fire which fills the entire universe. Try to understand the nature of this fire and its capacity to enter into us and to stir the very depths of our beings so that its properties become ours. Learn to absorb it, to soak it up, so that the heat of it melts and reshapes your old, rigid forms. In some areas we should work with water, for water has the power of transforming the earth and rocks within us. But where metal is concerned we have to use fire.

So learn to handle the power of heavenly fire. All too often, human beings allow themselves to he burned by the other kind of fire, astral fire, the fire of desire, which gives off quantities of smoke and`leaves heaps of ash. Heavenly fire produces no smoke and leaves no waste behind it. It produces only light, warmth and life. Unfortunately men and women prefer to light the devouring flames of astral fire and then they cry out because they get burned. It never occurs to anyone to doubt them. Nobody is surprised because everybody knows what it is like! But when it comes to lighting the inner, celestial fire there are not so many candidates.

There are three kinds of fire, or rather there are thousands of different kinds of fire, but it is simpler to put them into three different categories. The first category is physical: physical fire makes no distinction between the just and the unjust. It burns everything in its path indiscriminately. The second category is astral fire, which is Hell fire, and it has a special fondness for people who are full of passion and lust and evil designs. It is always ready to pounce on them and burn them up because they are just what it needs to feed its hungry flames. And then there is Heavenly fire which seeks out only those who are pure and full of light, and when it finds them, it too pounces on them, but to set them burning even brighter and transform them into true children of God, blazing with light and beauty like the sun.

Physical fire therefore does not choose, it burns whatever comes its way and does not distinguish the just from the unjust. That is not its business: its business is to burn. But the two other kinds of fire can choose. Divine fire will not descend indiscriminately. It is a bolt from the blue, like lighting, but it is not blind. Yes, you could say that it is a kind of thunderbolt: those who receive graces and blessings from Heaven are struck by a divine thunderbolt. The French use the expression '*coup de foudre*' (thunderbolt) to mean love at first sight. A young man might say, 'As soon as I saw her I had a "coup de foudre" ', and if this happens, unfortunately we know in advance that he is in for much suffering and sorrow. He may even be driven to murder. Why do some people have this overwhelming experience of love at first sight? It is because they need to suffer and through their suffering to learn a certain number of things. Others are overwhelmed by a different kind of thunderbolt: a thunderbolt from Heaven which leaves them in tears, too, but tears of ecstasy. Many saints and mystics have been given this grace. Read their lives and you will see how St. John of the Cross, little St. Thérèse and many others, experienced the 'coup de foudre' for Christ. Even some poets and painters have had this experience. To my mind no other grace can be compared to this heavenly thunderbolt of sacred fire. Nothing is more precious, nothing rarer or more wonderful. There is nothing to surpass it.

Now you must not believe that when someone has been struck by this thunderbolt he immediately knows and understands everything. Not at all. Heavenly fire does not necessarily nor automatically make us omniscient and all-powerful, it simply gives us the power to transform ourselves, so it is still up to us to collaborate with this fire in order to develop ideally, perfectly. Unfortunately it is possible to lose this grace, to lose the Holy Spirit and that is the greatest misfortune that could ever befall a human being, the most grievous loss a man can ever know. Many occultists, mystics and Initiates have been in possession of the sacred fire and then lost it, one way or another. Some have managed to win it back again, but at the cost of untold suffering and tears, repentance and unflagging labours. Heavenly fire has such a high degree of consciousness that it is almost as though it were insulted that someone could neglect it to the point of letting it slip away completely. He has to humble himself, shed many tears and plead for a long time before it consents to return to him. But once this happens, it anchors itself so firmly and puts down such strong roots deep inside a person that it can never again be uprooted!

I have had a lot of experiences and studied many cases in which fire was involved. In fact I keep up a constant dialogue with every kind of fire: inner fire and outer fire. Fire is the only thing I am interested in! When I was a child I used to light fires in barns and then, when I was older, I realized that I would do far better to leave physical fire alone and begin to light the inner fire, first of all in my own heart and then in the hearts of others.

And now my advice to you is this: put yourself in the presence of the rising sun every morning, knowing that it contains a spark, a flame from which you can light the fire in your own heart. It is like the Ceremony of Light in Orthodox churches on Easter morning: the pope lights a candle and, with this candle, lights the candle of the person nearest to him who, in turn, lights his neighbour's candle, and so on until the whole church is ablaze with light. A single candle is enough to spread light throughout the whole church. The symbolism of this ceremony is obvious. The sun, too, is a candle from which you can light your own little candle. Sometimes it takes years before your candle catches fire because inside you it is windy or raining, but one fine day it actually happens! Your candle catches fire and begins to give off a tiny light of its own. And then your neighbour exclaims, 'Ah, there's a light,' and he comes and lights his own candle from yours and then another one comes, and another and then another. And so it spreads and spreads and, one day, the whole world will be full of lighted candles.

Or perhaps you would like a rather more prosaic comparison: a man who uses a lighter to light his cigarette. It is not a very brilliant comparison but it serves my purpose. The sun is the flint (well, you have heard stranger things than that about the sun!) and you are holding a piece of iron. So, every morning you start striking your piece of iron against the flint and one day it produces a spark. The flint is always there, every day, but the bit of iron does not always turn up on time. So, keep your appointment with the sun and bring that bit of iron with you and strike it against the flint. In other words: put your will to work to produce a spark. It is up to you to do the striking.

It is always we who have to make the effort, not the sun. The sun has done all the work he needed to do a long time ago! It is we who have to go out to meet him and work to light our little candle from his great torch.

Is it all quite clear for you now? Have I interpreted the signs and symbols on the pages of Nature's great Book correctly?

Chapter 7

THE NAKED TRUTH

A few years ago, some people who ran a nudist camp invited me to visit them and see for myself what it was like. So, one day I went to their camp and of course I was the one who caused a sensation because I was the only one who had any clothes on! Gradually the campers came up to me: there were young girls and older women and men, and what is extraordinary is that when one finds oneself with so many people who are naked, one has no particular reaction. I admit this surprised me. I looked at all those people and thought to myself, 'There's really nothing to be scandalized about!' Judging from their attitudes and their expressions they all seemed to be perfectly natural and at ease. We sat down together for a while and several of them asked questions about various subjects and they all listened very attentively to what I had to say.

I know you are probably longing to ask me if I am in favour of nudism. Well, I am neither for nor against it, but I did notice a few things which could have been better. I had been told that as nudists have freed themselves from certain complexes they had a better chance of being healthy, well-balanced, even pure, and I wanted to see for myself if this was really so. Unfortunately, I found it was not entirely true. In the first place, they were bored because they did not have enough to do. But, above all, as they had no initiatic understanding of the nature and power of the elements: earth, water, air and light, the benefits they got from their nudity were very meagre. I also saw that they were not free from all kinds of desires and needs and that their nakedness was a way of satisfying those needs. Nudity, therefore, was not helping them to attain purity.

Purity is something more than being capable of taking all one's clothes off without feeling shame. Besides, purity does not only concern sexuality, it embraces all areas of life. If a person introduces purity into his intellect, he understands; when he introduces it into his will he becomes active and strong; when purity reigns in his physical body he is in good health, and when he is pure in heart and soul he becomes clairvoyant. As Jesus said, 'Blessed are the pure of heart for they shall see God.' So if you look at purity only from the angle of sexuality you will be missing the point.

Nudism is spreading, now, all over the world. There are a great many books and articles on the subject, but people do not have the essential knowledge they need in this area. As long as human beings do not know the truth about certain spiritual realities, nudism will not give them any of the advantages they expect from it: it will just be a question of a few experiments with little or no beneficial results.

It is good to want to commune with the forces of Nature, the air and sunshine, but as long as human beings are so limited in their understanding both of Nature and of themselves they will not benefit much from it. Their physical pores are exposed and open, perhaps, but their spiritual pores are closed because they do not know what it means to expose oneself to cosmic currents. So, even when they live naked in natural surroundings they do not profit much from the experience.

There is nothing bad in being naked. We all get undressed to have a bath and so on. When you are alone, at home, it is perfectly acceptable to be naked, it is only in front of others that it is considered unsuitable. The reason is not hard to find: as human beings are neither pure nor strong-willed enough to keep themselves in check, they have had to invent a certain number of rules to protect themselves from each other. But in actual fact there is nothing wrong in being nude. Besides, ask Nature if it infuriates her to see human beings wandering naked through her forests and along her seashores. She will surely reply, 'I don't mind one way or the other. If it makes them happy to be naked that's all right with me! Besides, when I sent them down to earth they didn't have any clothes on. If they have a reason for putting on clothes, that's their business. All I know is that when I made them they were naked.'

Men's and women's physical bodies are equipped with etheric antennae which enable them to communicate with Nature and receive certain forces and pick up messages. It follows, therefore, that if they expose their bodies to the elements in a forest or by the sea when they want to communicate and do some spiritual work with the earth, water, air or light, they have a much better chance of picking up and sending out signals and, consequently, of getting results. Sorcerers, and especially witches, have always known the power of nakedness and used it in making magic. Occult literature tells of many instances where witches were naked when they conjured up spirits or cast spells and curses, etc. Nudity attracts both good and evil forces and that is why it is dangerous to expose one's nude body if one is not sufficiently conscious and in control of oneself to defend oneself against the negative forces of darkness, and open oneself only to the forces of light.

Actually, men and women do not have the same attitude about nudity. On the whole, women are readier to show themselves in the nude than men, who are inclined to be ashamed to show their nakedness. But men like to see nude women and women like to be seen nude. At least, that is the way Nature made them, but for centuries now women have been taught that nudity is contrary to modesty and purity. However, it is obvious that many women have never accepted that idea. They may wear clothes in obedience to the rules but in their hearts they have never agreed with those rules because they go against their deepest nature. And it is not a question of vice or depravity. Women like to be seen nude. It is natural to them and they see nothing wrong in it.

It is not the fact of being nude that is reprehensible: it all depends on how a woman uses her nudity. When they realized that men were weak and easily troubled by their nudity, women saw a way to profit from it and so now they use their beauty to dominate and exploit men or to take revenge on them. This is so generalized in our day that, it is almost impossible to find a woman who is not aware of the power of her physical charm and who does not try to use it to lead men by the nose. It is only in this that they are guilty. If women are beautiful and have a lot of charm, so much the better. Who could possibly reproach them for it? But instead of using the powers Nature has given them to seduce men and keep them grovelling in filth, they must learn to use them to raise men's minds and hearts to higher things, to inspire and ennoble them and encourage them to strengthen their ties with Heaven.

The Mysteries teach that an Initiate must attain the contemplation of Isis unveiled. The purity and wisdom of an Initiate cause the veils of Isis – Nature – to fall away one by one until he beholds her in all her manifestations and knows all her secrets and the fullness of her beauty. Ideally speaking, therefore, a woman who is unclothed in the presence of her beloved symbolizes Isis unveiled to the gaze of an Initiate. In spite of their total ignorance about these things, people constantly reproduce Initiatic rites, the Mysteries of Isis, in their everyday lives. An example of this can be seen in the traditions surrounding a wedding: traditionnally, a bride is enveloped in veils until, on her wedding night, she allows her beloved to contemplate her unclothed body. Almost no one knows the origin nor the underlying meaning of such customs. In fact most people are content with the grossest, most inferior material aspect of this moment in their lives instead of preparing themselves to approach one of Nature's greatest mysteries. Nobody ever thinks they need to prepare themselves for marriage and that is why so many things go wrong.

Young newly-weds go off together for a 'honeymoon' and take it for granted that they are entitled to wallow in the pleasures of sex to the point of nausea. What a vile caricature of the eternal symbol of the Initiate preparing to celebrate his union with Isis, his beloved. No wonder young people today find neither love nor happiness in marriage! As long as they persist in such gross misconceptions there is no hope that they will ever find what they are looking and longing for. Ask a woman where her newly-wed daughter is, 'Oh, she's gone to Venice with her husband. They're spending their honeymoon there.' Honeymoon, indeed! And what are those two ignorant nitwits going to get up to? They are going to give themselves up completely to their pleasure until they are sick of it and of each other. And as they are both blind, neither of them will see the true beauty of the other. Neither of them will glimpse the soul or spirit of their partner, nor all the hidden glory within. All they will see will be some bare flesh, each other's bodies, physical matter. Poor, blind humanity!

An Initiate would never dream of wallowing in pleasure. He prepares himself for his union with Isis, his one love. He prepares himself for untold ecstasies. He knows that divine beauty and perfection are reflected in all manifestations of Nature but in no other manifestation is it more perfectly reflected than in the human body. Everywhere else it is scattered and fragmentary : the oceans are a part of the Cosmic Body, the rivers are another part, mountains and the sky are yet other parts. Only men and women reflect the whole Cosmic Body. God has condensed the entire universe in man and woman. And this is why, when an Initiate sees a human being who reflects the splendours of the universe more perfectly than others, he delights in contemplating that beauty and he uses it to strengthen his attachment to the beauty of God. He thinks to himself, 'Here is someone who speaks to me of the virtues of God Himself.' Contemplating him or her, he is in communion with divine beauty. Whereas, instead of being full of wonder at the beauty of Heaven reflected in their beloved, ordinary men and women fall upon them and misuse them for their own base pleasure. Like wild horses galloping through a field of flowers, they crush and destroy all that beauty with their hooves. If men and women were instructed in Initiatic Science they would admire the beauty of their beloved ten times more. And think what inspiration and strength they would gain this way and with what energy and determination they would return to their everyday tasks.

While I am on the subject I want to add something which I find very interesting. You know that the limbs and organs of the human body correspond with lines of force flowing through the cosmos. The various organs of the physical body were created in relation to these forces and several years ago, if you remember, some of you were surprised when I told you which areas of the cosmos were related to a woman's breasts. Everyone thinks that their only function is to feed her children. That is their physical function, it's true, but perhaps they have another function you do not know about. I told you that the left breast was related to the moon and the right breast to the Milky Way, and that if a woman was aware of these correspondences it would be a tremendous benefit to her in her spiritual advancement. Unfortunately, most of the time she is totally unaware that she is related in this way, not only to the whole of Nature in general but also to all other human beings in the world. But even if she is not aware of it, this etheric, magnetic communication still exists, and her two breasts give and receive something from the cosmos. Not very long after I had talked about this, I visited a museum in Spain and came across a painting by some obscure artist, which portrayed a nude woman with a moon on the left breast and the Milky Way flowing from the right breast. I must say I was astounded and delighted to see this illustration and confirmation of an Initiatic truth. The painter must certainly have had some knowledge of Initiatic Science.

The bodies of men and women epitomize the universe as a whole and the disciple must learn to look at them with awe and wonder and, above all, to use them as a stimulus for a renewed attachment to the sublime world on high. If he has this attitude, not only will he glorify the Lord, but he will advance rapidly on the path of evolution. He will be in a position to learn all of Nature's secrets, for if Isis is no longer forced to endure rape and violence in her body, she will unveil herself to his gaze. It is as though she murmurs to herself, 'My lover is gentle and attentive. His love is full of respect and admiration. I shall reveal myself to him.' And in this way the truth is laid bare before him, for Isis is Truth. His spirit will perceive the naked truth, truth as it really is above, not below. For here below, truth appears to us wrapped in veils and illusions, 'maya'. Truth reveals itself only to one who has the right attitude toward the mysteries of love.

To behold Isis unveiled, therefore, is to behold Truth. This is why the Initiates spoke of knowing the 'naked Truth', Truth stripped of all its veils.

But what are these veils? They are seven in number and they correspond to the seven levels of being: physical, etheric, astral, mental, causal, buddhic and atmic. When the seventh veil falls away, the Divine Mother, Mother Nature herself, is revealed in all her nakedness, in her subtlest and purest form, totally one with the Spirit.

If you want to know someone in this life try to know him, himself, and not just his clothes or veils. To do this you have to rise to where his spirit, his higher Self, dwells. You can truly know him only if you know him on that level. As long as you persist in seeing only his veils, the exterior appearance, you will end by tiring of him, whereas if you discover the Self concealed by the outer wrappings you will never tire of him: you will have found an inexhaustible source of joy. And this, mind you, is what I do with you. If I did not look at you that way I would have tired of you ages ago! I would certainly have concluded, 'There's nothing interesting here. Just the same old faces all the time!' It is just as well, isn't it, that I do not think that way! I 'undressed' you all a long time ago, the way most men 'undress' the women they meet. But don't misunderstand me!

No one has ever correctly interpreted this tendency on the part of men to undress a woman in order to see her as she is. It is a natural instinct given to men which incites them not to be content with outer appearances, but to look further and higher to where a woman is truly naked: in the realm of perfect purity, light and beauty. On the highest level there is nothing shameful in this. It is not a woman's physical body we contemplate, her hair or her breasts, but her soul, the Divinity. All human beings are aware of certain instincts in themselves but they never try to see beyond the lowest, most earthly manifestations of reality. They never interpret Nature's language. And, as they cling to the physical manifestations rather than to the sublime realities underlying them, they give up the struggle and become mired in their lower nature, and that's the end of them.

So when I say I have undressed you, don't misunderstand me: I simply mean that I am not content to know you only on the physical plane. I want to see you also on the divine level of your being, and on that level I see you as sons and daughters of God. Then the sight of you is extraordinarily beautiful, I rejoice in it and the stream of life-forces is set in motion and flows between us. Why not learn to do the same? Of course, we cannot do without physical form, but it is incapable of satisfying us indefinitely. We should regard it simply as a springboard. The physical form is like a bottle which has no intrinsic value: its only value is as a protection for the perfume it contains. It is the perfume that is valuable, because it is the quintessence of life. So, get into the habit of dwelling not on outward appearances and forms but on the vibrant inner spirit which diffuses light and life and creates a multitude of worlds. If you do that you will never know disappointment, but if you do not, sooner or later you will be bitterly disillusioned.

So far, you have only a glimmering of the tremendous secrets contained in the word 'nudity'. To be nude is to be stripped of all false conceptions and of all lust. Only truth is nude and to attain true nudity, therefore, we have to free ourselves of everything that is opaque, inert, coarse and impervious to the divine dimension. Only when we have attained this nudity can we soar to great heights and pick up the messages of wisdom and love that are being beamed toward us from Heaven.

The reason why so many people get so little out of meditation is that they try to rise to sublime heights without first taking off their dirty, tattered old clothes, symbolically speaking. How can their antennae possibly pick up anything that way? We have to be naked, that is divested of our cupidity, self-interest and prejudices. If we denude ourselves, then we can rise to higher levels and the more we renounce, the higher we shall rise. After our meditation, we come down again and have to put on our clothes again and go to work on the physical level. Clothes are necessary on earth, but not in Heaven. Heaven appreciates only those who are 'nude'.

Now you have some idea of what a magnificent symbol the Initiates of old gave us when they spoke of the 'naked truth', of 'Isis unveiled'.

Chapter 8

BUILDING A HOUSE

As I have often said, the actions and gestures of our everyday lives contain many lessons for us and we should apply ourselves to deciphering them. At the moment, for instance, you are helping to build our new dining-hall, but you have never reflected on the lessons you could draw from this work.

When you want to build a house, where do you begin? You begin with an idea in your mind. Your house exists, first of all, only on the invisible, mental level. Later, you put your idea on paper and draw the plans: this is the first manifestation on the physical level. Once your plans are complete, you start buying the building materials and, finally, you hire some workmen to come and build your house for you according to your specifications. So there are three, distinct stages: the plans, obtaining the building materials, and the actual construction work.

And once the building work begins, what is the first thing you work on? The roof? Of course not. You begin with the foundations, the groundwork. You think this is obvious, don't you? Well, it is not so obvious as it may seem. For some people it is not obvious at all; in fact very few really understand. But to get back to your house: once you have laid the foundations you can start putting up the walls and, finally, you put on the roof. So, for the outside, the framework of the house, you work from the bottom up. But what about the interior decorating: do you begin by polishing the floor? No, you begin with the ceiling, next you do the walls, and the floor comes last. So, for the inside of the house you work from the top down. And the final stage, when the actual building work is finished, is the decoration, the aesthetic side: you hang pictures on the walls, curtains in the windows, etc.

On the outside, therefore, we work from the bottom up and on the inside we work from the top down. So a house can teach us how to work with the two currents of evolution and involution. The work of building and decorating a house is symbolized by the two interlaced triangles which form the figure known as Solomon's Seal or the Star of David. It is a symbol which contains a wealth of meaning, it reveals how God created the world and how we, in turn, should work. The very first lesson we can learn from it is that we should not try to use the same methods in our outer life as in our inner life, that on the physical plane we have to work from the bottom up and for the inner, spiritual life we have to begin at the top and work downwards. Does this surprise you?

If you want to succeed on the physical level you have to work according to the laws of evolution and begin with the solid, material dimensions, gradually working your way up to more subtle levels. It is quite the reverse if you undertake to work on the psychic, interior level. Here you have to begin on the highest level, by all that is most subtle, luminous and divine, and finish with what is tangible and concrete. But how many know how to work like that? When it comes to building a house, of course, there is no problem but when it is a question of applying the same laws to one's own life, it does not seem quite so obvious.

To ensure results in the material world, you have to begin by building a solid, durable base. Whereas if you want results in the spiritual dimension you have to begin by making sure you have a good roof, otherwise even your foundations will crumble. In the spiritual dimension everything is reversed. It is as though the foundations were above and the roof below. You have to build things in your head, therefore, before trying to carry them out in the physical dimension and, since it takes a very long time for spiritual constructions to materialize on the physical plane, you have to work at them for years if you want them ever to be manifested physically.

This movement from top to bottom teaches us how God created the world. To create, God had to manifest Himself; He had to 'go out of' Himself and 'descend' to the material level. But this first downward movement, which is called involution, is followed by an upward movement by which God 'reintegrates' Himself and which is called evolution. In the first step God goes out of Himself to create worlds and in a second step He moves back and, as it were, reabsorbs all things into Himself. But these two movements take billions of years to accomplish.

The involutionary movement is from the top downwards (or from the centre outwards), whereas the evolutionary movement is from the bottom upwards (or from the outer edge towards the centre). Involution preceded evolution. Involution is a process of materialization whereas evolution, on the contrary, is a process of dematerialization. In Nature, these two opposing movements can constantly be seen working together: they converge and interact and their interaction engenders all forms of life. New forms are constantly being created in the physical dimension of space by the convergence and interaction of these two currents originating in God Himself. There is no spirit and no matter; there is only life flowing from the centre to the outer periphery and back to the centre again. Physical forms become more and more subtle as they get closer to the centre and more and more densely material as they move out from the centre towards the periphery. So the great circulatory current of Life is just this: forms moving inwards and becoming more immaterial and others moving outwards, becoming more solid.

Where else can we see the two processes of involution and evolution at work? Birth is involution: a child comes down into the material plane. Death is evolution: a man retreats from the material level and moves inwards towards the Spirit. When we undress at night, that is evolution and when we get dressed in the morning, that is involution. You only have to look at what you do when you get dressed: some garments have to be put on from the top downwards and others from the bottom up. You see, the two complementary movements of involution and evolution are present even in such commonplace gestures as dressing and undressing. But nobody ever notices or thinks about this.

Initiatic Science teaches that the two currents, involution and evolution, were operative in forming human beings. To start with, human beings had only heads. The heart, lungs, stomach and limbs were added much later. But at that stage man was not yet in the visible world. His head had not even been materialized, it was a kind of ball of fire floating in the etheric plane. Man began to materialize only when his feet were formed. In fact it was his feet which materialized first and, later, his legs, thighs, genitals, solar plexus, stomach and so on, up to his head. The head was the last part of man to become material although it was the first to be formed on the invisible level, whereas his feet, which were the last to be formed on the invisible level, were the first to appear on the physical level.

The two currents of evolution and involution can equally be found in astrology. If you run through the signs of the Zodiac beginning with Aries, Taurus, Gemini, Cancer, etc., you are moving in the direction of involution, and that is how human beings were formed: beginning with the head. Aries represents the head, for each sign of the Zodiac corresponds to a part of the human body. But the equinoctial point moves in the opposite direction, starting with Pisces, Aquarius, Capricorn, Sagittarius, Scorpio and so on. This is the evolutionary movement and it follows the order in which the different organs of the human body materialized. And now, if you look at the movement of the Zodiac in relation to that of the planets you will see the same opposition: the constellations of the Zodiac move through the sky in the following order: Aries, Taurus, Gemini and so on, whereas the planets move in the opposite direction. The planets, therefore, move with the currents of involution and the Zodiac with the currents of evolution.

But I do not want to prolong this diversion into astrology: I ask you simply to remember that if you want to succeed in the spiritual life you must begin by building the roof, next the walls and, last, the foundations, because in the invisible world the roof is really the base or foundation, the ground on which we must build; but we shall continue to call it the roof so as not to get everything mixed up! So, when I say that in the invisible world you have to begin with the roof, this means, amongst other things, that before you begin to pose as a sage, a prophet, a clairvoyant or a healer, you must first study for a very long time and be deeply attached to the Lord so as to be firmly rooted in the divine dimension. It takes years and years of patience, study and hard work before one can begin to manifest authentic spiritual gifts.

Unfortunately, most people who embark on the spiritual life want to let everyone know about it at once. They make themselves ridiculous by trying to look inspired and superior and seem to think that they can immediately guide and instruct others. In fact they can be quite dangerous for others. You must realize that one cannot manifest authentic spiritual gifts if one has not spent long years working, meditating and praying. What you should do is work and pray and let things manifest themselves! What you are will manifest itself without your talking about it. In fact you will not be able to help it, it will do so in spite of you.

Allow the invisible world to manifest itself by shining through your expression, your eyes, your face, your voice, your gestures. Some people come and tell me, 'I've been sent from Heaven. I have a very special mission. You must listen to me and follow me!' Well, this only shows that they do not know the laws of the spiritual world. Even if you are Christ Himself, you should never say so! Never try to assert yourself. Wait until your gifts and qualities command respect of themselves and, gradually, others will be obliged to recognize them and speak for you. This is how the truly spiritual man functions. For years and years he works and builds on the invisible plane, without talking about it and then, one day, even the most obtuse begin to see that something has been built. But try to convince people that you are the Messiah or the Blessed Virgin, they will lock you up! Just as they would lock up someone who was crazy enough to try and put a roof on his house before laying the foundations. If you tell other people that you are very rich or very skilful they will not take your word for it. They will believe you only when you have been able to prove it to them, when they have seen for themselves. If what they see is only the first beginnings of the house you are building, they are not going to be very impressed. And the same holds good in the spiritual life, except that people who are equipped to make judgments on the physical level are not so clearsighted when it comes to spiritual things, so you have to work far longer.

Now let's see what else a house can teach us: as I told you, when you decorate a room you have to follow a certain order: first the ceiling, then the walls, including the doors and windows and, last, the floor. And we have to follow the same order in our psychic life: thought comes first (symbolically we hang the lamps from the ceiling and turn on the light); next comes feeling: we feel whether our ideas and plans are right and good, and finally we act and put our ideas into effect.

When you act you do not walk about on the ceiling or the walls, but on the floor. Ceiling, walls and floor correspond to the three realms of thought, feeling and action. Light, that is wisdom, intelligence and knowledge, comes from above. The area of feeling is represented by the walls, on which we hang paintings, mirrors and all kinds of pretty things, and the world of action is the floor, on which we walk and move about, the level on which we work. 'And what about the windows?' you may ask. The windows represent our eyes and so we have to wash our windows in order to see everything clearly. There you have another page from the living Book of Nature, the book that we shall never finish studying.

A lot of people begin with the floor and, as we have just seen, the floor represents action. They act first, without thinking, and the result is, of course, that they come into conflict with other people or things. Then, as this causes suffering and inconvenience, they realize that something is wrong and they begin to think and draw some conclusions. How much better it would have been if they had done a little thinking before launching into action. People often have the mistaken idea that a kind of 'trial run' will help them to draw valid conclusions, but this is not so. The only way to arrive at correct conclusions is to think things out in advance: this is self-evident.

On the physical level, therefore, we have to follow the evolutionary current, whereas on the psychic level we use the methods of involution, the methods of the spirit. When a man shows his prospective wife his cars and houses and all his degrees and diplomas, she sees that he has the means to provide for her comfort and wellbeing.

And when a customer goes into a shop to buy something, the salesman is not interested in knowing if he is intelligent or kind, but if he is going to get out his wallet – and if there is plenty of money in it! Where Heaven is concerned the situation is quite different: even if you possess houses and great estates on earth, even if you own several banks, the heavenly gate-keepers may well refuse you admittance, saying, 'We don't know who you are. You haven't begun work on your roof up here yet!' A man may be extremely wealthy, powerful and highly respected on the physical level, but he will never be respected, admired or loved in the spiritual world until he begins to form virtues and entertain pure and noble thoughts within himself.

Some people imagine that because they have succeeded in the material, visible world they will necessarily be a success on the spiritual level also. But they are sadly mistaken. These are two, quite distinct areas. Others, who have managed to develop virtues and spiritual qualities, imagine that this qualifies them for success in the material world, but they too are mistaken. Their virtues are invisible and, besides, materialists have no respect for them anyway. If you want to be understood and appreciated on the material level, you have to work with the evolutionary forces, that is, establish solid foundations here, on earth.

Whereas, if you want to succeed in the invisible world and to be made welcome and protected by spirits from on high, if you want revelations and ecstasy and if you want to possess the fullness of life, you have to work with the forces of involution and begin by being rooted in Heaven. Obviously, the best of all is to work with both lines of force in order to earn recognition both in Heaven and on earth: Heaven will recognize the Initiate and men will recognize someone who is capable of achievements on earth.

Unfortunately there are not too many examples of this. What we see, for the most part, are people who are highly qualified on the physical level but totally ignorant on the spiritual level, or 'mystics' who walk around with their roofs suspended in mid-air and who are quite incapable of achieving anything practical. So this is why the disciples of an Initiatic School must learn the laws of the spiritual world in order to build their home on solid foundations on high. At the same time they must be able to manifest on the physical level by their work and their responsible behaviour. They must become well-balanced, perfect citizens of both worlds.

So now you see all the lessons contained in a house!

Chapter 9

RED AND WHITE

On the first day of spring each year, in Bulgaria and in most other Slavonic countries, people wear two little red and white pompoms in their buttonholes. Nobody knows exactly where this age-old custom comes from, but the two little pompoms have profound symbolic significance in alchemy.

In alchemical texts you will find references to the Red Man and the White Woman, who may also be represented as the sun and the moon, and gold and silver are the corresponding metals. But in their treatises, alchemists were always very secretive about two things: the exact nature of the substance they used in the Great Work and the degree of heat reached in the course of the Work. The substance was designated by many different, often very bizarre, names (for example: brass, orpiment, iron, magnesia, moon spittle, virgin's milk, minery and so on) and we are told that it was composed of two elements. The Work properly speaking started only when these two elements began to be cooked together at some unspecified temperature.

The precise moment at which the Great Work should be undertaken was determined in accordance with astrological phenomena: just as the sun entered Aries, that is to say in the first few days of spring, and with the moon in Taurus. This is the most auspicious moment to start, because the sun is exalted in Aries and the moon in Taurus. The sun symbolizes the active, masculine principle whereas the moon represents the passive, feminine principle. In alchemy, red symbolizes man and white, woman. So the two little red and white balls are symbols of the two principles perpetually at work in Nature.

Alchemical Work begun in the first days of spring produces two powders, one red and one white. The red powder has the power to transmute base metals into gold and the white powder transmutes base metals into silver. But these two little red and white balls are to be found in Nature, also. First of all in the red and white corpuscles of the blood and also, with a slightly different nuance in the colour, in the yolk and white of an egg. So you see, if you wear the red and white balls in your buttonhole you, too, will be alchemists, but unconscious alchemists, because you still do not know how to transform the base metals within you into gold and silver. This can only be done by love and wisdom. The transmutation of metals into gold and silver is an alchemical process which must be made to happen in the three worlds and not only in the physical dimension. If you want your thoughts to be turned to silver, you have to use light and wisdom and, if you want your feelings to turn to gold, you have to use the warmth of love.

The moment when the sun enters Aries is of primary importance for alchemists, for it is then that the sun – the masculine principle – acts most powerfully on the earth – the feminine principle. The earth receives and absorbs the sun's rays and begins to produce leaves, flowers and fruit. Spring is the Philosophers' Stone, the Life which renews and rejuvenates the whole of Nature. The fire of the sun acts on the First Matter, the earth, to give it life. This is the alchemical symbolism of spring. In winter the earth is cold and barren, but once its substance has been 'cooked' for a while by the heat of the sun's rays, all its hidden treasures begin to come to the surface.

The alchemists observed what took place on the earth and understood how Nature worked to transform and transfigure everything: that which is dead, black and shrivelled, comes alive and displays its colourful beauty. Why do you suppose that the feast of the Resurrection was celebrated in the spring? Yes, Easter is also an alchemical symbol. In the spring, Nature is vibrant with renewed vitality, everything rises from the dead, and the sages of old who pored over the laws of Nature found that the same phenomena must occur in man. For the sun and moon and the vegetable kingdom are also present in man, and in man, too, everything can be transformed and brought back to life – sometimes much more rapidly than in Nature.

Every day the organs of your physical body are busy transforming quantities of matter into gold and silver, that is to say, into red and white corpuscles in your blood. And they find this raw material in Nature in four different forms or states: fire, air, water and earth. When you take in light, air, water and solid food, you are manufacturing gold inside your body. The very fact that you are able to move about, talk and work is proof enough of this. And if you are capable of maintaining and prolonging your own life this way, it means that, in a way, you too are alchemists.

God exists, in the first place, in the igneous or fiery state. Hermes Trismegistus was speaking about gold when he said, 'The Sun is its father and the Moon its mother, the Wind has carried it in its belly and the Earth is its nurse.' Gold is produced by the sun. Each one of the sun's rays is pure gold and the moon is the reflection of that gold. The sun's rays travel through the air and into the bowels of the earth where they condense, transforming themselves into the metal we call gold. The sun, therefore, manufactures etheric gold and the earth condenses it into metal. In the sun it is in too volatile a state to be fixed; this can only be done when it reaches the bowels of the earth and it is the earth that supplies the materials needed for this fixation to take place. So this is why I keep telling you to get into the habit of contemplating the sun, remembering that it is gold and, little by little, that gold will sink in and condense within you.

It is entirely up to you to persuade the sun to open and shower you with his treasures. The more intensely loving your gaze, the richer the harvest you will reap of particles of gold in the form of light, wonderment, joy, peace, health, activity and strength. If the alchemists sometimes called the raw material they used 'iron', it is an indication that it was capable of generating great force and dynamic energy.

The alchemists tell us that, before it reaches the red and white phase, matter has to go through a dark phase. This darkness is like going through a subterranean passage before emerging into daylight again, or like winter: it is a period of preparation. Sometimes the alchemists likened this stage of the process to what they called 'the black cadaver'. The cadaver represented matter which dies and putrifies, and out of that black putrefaction emerges first the white and then the red.

Jesus said, 'Unless a grain of wheat falls to the ground and dies, it remains only a single seed. But if it dies it produces many seeds.' In its black phase, alchemists' matter was known as 'crow'; when it reached the white stage it was known as 'Diana's dove', and in its red stage it was called the 'Phoenix'. The Phoenix represents the ultimate, perfected state of the raw material. In between the white and the red stages it goes through a whole range of intermediary colours: green, purple, etc., known as the 'Peacock's Tail'. But I will not go into this question of colours, it would only distract us from our subject and it would not even be useful for you.

An Initiate, a great Master, a Saviour of mankind, has to live through the same phases as the material used by alchemists in their work. They have to die in order to rise again. And Jesus, who was crucified and rose from the dead, is a symbol of the Philosophers' Stone. In fact the alchemists believed that everything in Scripture had alchemical significance. All the stories recounted in the Bible correspond to one or another phase of the Great Work. Let us take just one example, the massacre of the Innocents by Herod:

Nicholas Flamel considers that the way in which Herod's soldiers snatched the babies from their mothers' bosoms in order to shed their blood was symbolic. He says that the children's blood was collected in a bowl in which were steeped the sun and the moon. Each alchemist chose a particular passage from Scripture to symbolize the different phases of the Great Work. Some chose Daniel's dream in which he saw four great beasts emerging from the sea; others, Nebuchadnezzar's dream of a great statue made of gold, silver, bronze, iron and clay; still others, the passage which tells of how Elisha the prophet cured Naaman of his leprosy by ordering him to go and wash himself seven times in the Jordan.

All through the Bible, therefore, are passages which can, be interpreted as symbols of the alchemists Great Work and even some of the events in our own lives can be interpreted in the same way. For instance, if you are the victim of calumny you become 'black', then circumstances change, you are exonerated from the slanderous accusations and this represents the white stage; you 'rise from the dead' and begin to enjoy the fruits of your labours: it is the red stage.

Now, I am not telling you all this with the idea of encouraging you to start trying to produce gold, it is not gold that should interest you. My aim is, rather, to help you to open your eyes and renew your sense of wonderment before the works of Nature. Study Nature in all its multifarious phenomena and you will soon feel a great light dawning within you. Every morning, when you contemplate the sun in its rising, you can drink deeply of the Elixir of Everlasting Life. But the whole of Nature, the sun and also the air, the plants and the very soil of the earth offer us the same immortal Elixir.

Now I would like to add a few words about the two little red and white balls we wear in our buttonholes in spring, but I am not at all sure how you will understand me.

In alchemy, matter passes through the white phase before it becomes red. In presenting things this way alchemists reversed the situation which prevails on the physical plane, where man is white and woman red. Incandescent white corresponds to the sun and red to the earth. In the old days there was a custom in some countries, which some of you may know: on the morning after his wedding night the bridegroom was supposed to appear at his bedroom window, while all his family and friends gathered below, and showed them a piece of linen which proved the virginity of his bride, and this proof was greeted with applause and song. In the union of a man and a woman we have the two colours, white and red: the man provides the white and the woman the red. And now you can think what you please! If you are shocked, remember it is not my fault. It is Nature who arranged things this way.

When alchemists speak of the Red Man and the White Woman, therefore, they are deliberately switching the symbols and I am not going to tell you why. In the past, the Initiates concealed the deepest truths in similar ways. The encounter between a man and a woman is the starting point of an alchemical process: the creation of a child. Think what a wondrous thing this is. The birth of a child is one of the most extraordinary events to occur in Nature.

Spring is the sun's nuptial union with the earth, the beginning of the Work. In spring, Nature brings a multitude of children into the world. Without the father (the sun), the mother could not produce any fruit. But all these cosmic phenomena also exist within human beings. There, it is the soul that is the bride and the spirit that is the bridegroom. On the first day of spring, if the soul abandons herself to the Divine Spirit she will be impregnated, but if she refuses to surrender herself to Him, nothing will happen and she will remain barren.

In the spring the earth lays herself open to the rays of the sun, but this same cosmic process of fecundation is enacted in all spheres. The Holy

Spirit, too, invites you to lay yourselves open to Him in order to receive His gifts of wisdom and love, for the Spirit of God can impregnate your souls just as the sun impregnates the earth. It is not easy, however, to attract the Holy Spirit. In the Gospels it says, 'The wind blows wherever it pleases. You hear its sound, but you cannot tell where it comes from or where it is going...' The spirit will come only into a soul which has prepared itself to make Him welcome, with the greatest possible respect, love and devotion. When the Spirit enters that soul, then the Infant Christ is born: this is the Philosophers' Stone with which the Initiate works wonders. In order to be visited by the Spirit, the soul must be like a young virgin: only after long hours spent in loving meditation and contemplation of the tastes and preferences of her Prince Charming does she set out to attract his attention and to delight him with her winning smile and graceful mien. In order to receive the Holy Spirit, all human beings, even men, must become women. But what does it mean to be a woman? It means to be an Aeolian harp, vibrating at the slightest breath of wind. Woman, the soul, is a harp, and man, the spirit, is the hand which caresses the strings of the harp.

The Apostles received the Holy Spirit because their souls, like women, had prepared themselves with loving respect of His coming. The same law can be seen at work on the physical plane: it is only really feminine women who attract men because men are positive and emissive and women are receptive. No one wants to marry a virago unless it be a sage who, like Socrates, is looking for another Xanthippe on whom to practise his virtue! Some wise men, who want to become stronger, choose to marry shrews but the spirits of light will never wed a shrewish soul! They are sensible only to the appeal of truly loving, feminine souls, full of trust and adoration. Anyone who is incapable of becoming such a woman in relation to the Holy Spirit is condemned to barrenness.

For hundreds and even thousands of years, human beings considered a barren woman to be under a curse. In fact, this attitude towards sterility stems from a knowledge of far deeper realities. If the earth is sterile it becomes a desert. If his soul is sterile, a human being can never receive the breath of inspiration. So if the woman, the feminine principle in each one of us, is sterile, if our soul is sterile, we shall never be blessed with any form of creativity. In the Book of Genesis it says that God told man to 'Increase and multiply', and this command has almost always been understood to apply solely on the physical plane, for the procreation of children. But it also concerns the human soul which must be fertile and give birth to its own magnificent brood: inspiration and enthusiasm.

The great thing in all this is to understand the lessons Nature has to offer. At the beginning of spring the earth lays itself open to receive the sun. In the same way, man has to learn to lay open his soul and when he does so he will experience a joy such as he has never known before. If a man is insensible to that joy of Nature pulsating with life all around him, if he does not feel the rays of the spiritual sun penetrating his soul just as the physical sun penetrates the earth, it is because he has still not understood the meaning of spring.

All these truths are drawn from the great treasure-house of eternal truths. The invisible world has given me a special gift for explaining them simply and clearly, which is why I always use the same explanations. Possibly, in the future, you will read books about these same subjects and then you will be struck by the simplicity of my explanations compared to the abstract, complicated explanations of other authors.

Chapter 10

THE RIVER OF LIFE

At some time in their lives, surely everyone must have seen a river, but very few, I believe, have ever paused to reflect on the correspondence between a river and a human life. And yet, inherent to the notion of a river are all the elements we need to find answers to our problems. However, before we can do this we have to see all the manifestations of Nature as living, coherent elements of a highly, organized whole in which every detail is meaningful.

A river is a symbol of life. Its source is always high up in the mountains. It is a link, an intermediary between the mountain and the ocean, sea or lake into which it flows. A river joins what is above to what is below. Along the banks of every river, civilizations arise and prosper because a river causes life to flow and circulate: where water flows, Life flows too. If you study history you will see that along the banks of the great rivers of the world there have been great civilizations. On the other hand, when a river dries up civilization also disappears.

Now, if we interpret this concept of a river, you will be astonished to see what a wealth of meaning it contains. A river flows down from its source in the mountains to the valleys and plains below. Its water, gushing in a crystal-clear stream from a mountain spring, flows through all kinds of regions and becomes more and more polluted because the inhabitants of those regions are not particularly scrupulous about throwing their waste into the river. They never think of others, downstream, who are going to have to drink the water they have polluted. Besides, the others do exactly the same, so that by the time the river reaches the plains, anyone who drinks its waters, is in danger of sudden death!

What does a river represent? It is one of the most profound symbols in Nature. It symbolizes the Cosmic River described in the Book of Revelation: the River of Life which slakes the thirst of all God's creatures. The River of Life flows down to us through the realms of the celestial hierarchies (Seraphim, Cherubim, Thrones, Dominions, Powers, Virtues, Principalities, Archangels and Angels) and each angelic order contributes to its life-giving waters their own particular qualities and virtues. It flows through the dwelling-places of the Glorified Souls, the Prophets, Great Masters and Initiates, nourishing and vivifying all those who have attained wisdom, purity and sanctity. But when it reaches still lower levels, the level of ordinary human beings, the river of life suffers exactly the same fate as a physical river into which people throw their rubbish.

From its source to the sea, a river represents a hierarchy and that hierarchy can equally well be ourselves, from our higher Selves, in the mountains, down to the lowest levels of our being, our mental, astral and physical bodies. Without realizing it, human beings are continually throwing the filth of their thoughts, feelings and actions into the River of Life so that they are all forced to feed on each other's refuse. The world is like a highly polluted river into which everybody pours their resentment, anger and evil desires.

Just like water, life is coloured, polluted or purified, according to what it encounters in the regions it flows through. Pure or polluted, life is still life, but it has different degrees and depending on the regions it flows through and the creatures who dwell along its banks, it possesses various properties. People do not all receive the same life from the river. Very often one hears people say, 'What do you expect? There's nothing you can do about it. That's life!' Yes, of course, that may be life, but what kind of life are they talking about? The life of a toad or a wild boar? The life of a crocodile? Or the life of an angel? Life which comes from God has different degrees and it flows down, even into subterranean regions to nourish the lower levels of beings. Yes, even devils are nourished by the River of Life. What did you think? Where else could they get life from? There would have to be another God with another life; in other words God would have a rival as powerful or even more powerful than He. But that is nonsense: there is only one God and He nourishes all creatures, even devils. The only thing is that devils do not receive the purest nourishment. They have to make do with left-overs and the left-overs are already dirty, polluted and poisoned. In fact this is the appointed lot of all subterranean creatures, they have to be content to nibble the scraps that fall from the table of divine life.

It is quite easy to understand this: just look at how beggars on this earth forage through the rubbish bins of the rich in the hope of finding something to eat. The poor wretches are there to teach us a lesson and their message is this: 'Look at us! We didn't want to learn or work at improving ourselves and now we're reduced to hunting for a few crusts and peelings thrown out by the rich. We're like creatures of the underworld who have to make do with the peelings left over from celestial life.' Yes, beggars and tramps have a message and a lesson for everybody, but how many understand their language?

Some of you may be surprised and rather shocked at the idea that God nourishes the creatures who dwell in Hell. But we only have to reason a little: where did these lower creatures, the devils who torment human beings, come from? From where did they get life? Only God can create and distribute life. If other beings could do this they would be as powerful as God. But, in fact, God has no rivals. No one can stand up to Him. And, above all, He does not need human beings to help Him combat the forces of evil. He alone has all power over life and His generosity is such that He allows no creature to die completely, even the lowest of the low. And the reason is that they are all at His service.

Yes, indeed! Devils are at the service of God. When a human being needs to be taught a lesson, God does not administer it Himself, He tells His avenging servants – the devils – to go and find such and such a person and shake him up a bit to make him think! And if the Lord expects His servants to work for Him, He obviously has to feed them. Of course, it is not the choicest morsels, nor the biggest, which fall from Heaven for them. But at least they do receive some nourishment. And that is how I explain God's generosity which implies the extraordinary hope that even these fallen creatures will, one day, repent and purify themselves and return to God. I know you do not believe me but it is true! People are so cruel, they do not even want the devils to change their ways and improve. They think they should burn in Hell for all eternity. But God does not think like that. He thinks of getting them to mend their ways and come back to Him. But as His patience is infinite He is in no hurry, so there are still plenty of devils around to torment human beings. But the day will come – and it is not very far off – when they will no longer be free to torment men; they will be shackled.

I can see that you are wondering how I know all this and the answer is that I know it because I have read it. And where did I read it? Oh, not in any book written by a human hand. I have no confidence at all in books written by human beings, I have been disappointed too often by all the mistakes and incoherencies in them, so I never waste my time reading them any more. The only book I read is the book of living Nature and it was there that I discovered that God's love and God's life reach down even into the depths of the earth and the bottom of the deepest abyss. Even there, there are still a few crumbs of life, otherwise no creature could continue to exist in those regions. You may object, 'But it is man who creates life.'

No, you are mistaken. Life comes from God, the only thing man can do is to transmit life, he cannot create it. If he could he would never need to die. Man only hands on life to another for a limited period of time. He is not a creator of life.

But, let's get back to the idea of a river. As I was saying, the river of divine life flows down into the depths of the earth. And it is down there that it is cleansed of all the impurities it has picked up on its way. It flows through underground filter beds and then goes upwards again, but under a different form. Exactly like water which descends from the mountain-side: when it gets to the sea it is dirty, murky and polluted, but under the influence of the sun's rays it evaporates and rises above the ocean where it becomes cloud, then falls back to earth again in the form of rain, snow or dew. The same cycle can be seen in the circulation of the blood: clean blood flows from the lungs to the heart which pumps it out to the other organs of the body. On its way it collects all kinds of waste materials and then goes back to the lungs to be cleansed and purified again. Blood as it circulates through our bodies; water as it circulates under the surface of the earth; these are pages which we have read in the book of Nature. Nature is God's book, His own masterpiece in which He expresses Himself, and His laws are all written down there for anyone who takes the trouble to learn to read. But human beings are not interested in studying the book of Nature, they prefer books written by diseased and misshapen human authors!

A little while ago I spoke about beggars and tramps, and in this connection I would like to show you in more detail some of the correspondences we can find between the outer and the inner life. When people are very well off they can afford to go to the best restaurants and eat fresh food of the very best quality, whereas the poor have to go to cheap little restaurants where they can get soup or cheap stew which is often made from the left-overs of the smart restaurants. And then there are those who cannot afford to buy a meal at all – the destitute – and all they can get to eat is a few crusts and scraps collected from rubbish bins. So you see, those who have plenty of money can buy the freshest, most nourishing food whereas the poor are obliged to eat other people's leavings. Exactly the same phenomenon can be seen on the spiritual or psychic level, only, on this level, it will probably be the rich of this world who have. to hunt for their food in rubbish bins!

In the inner life the same hierarchies exist as in outer life. When a human being harbours only noble thoughts and feelings, his soul feeds on heavenly foods, whereas someone who is full of spite and lust and his own base desires, sinks down to the lower reaches of life and takes his place among the destitute. He cannot afford to buy a meal in the best restaurants of the spiritual world. He is obliged to eat other people's left-overs and he will not be able to form a pure, luminous spiritual body for himself because the food he eats is soiled and lifeless. One must be rich in virtues of all kinds to be able to eat in celestial restaurants. If you do not want to eat other people's left-overs, instead of remaining bogged down in the lower regions, there is only one solution and that is to rise to great heights. This is the most important secret of spiritual life. Just as one has to go up into the mountains to find pure, unsullied water, so you have to go up to the Source if you want to drink of the crystal-clear waters of divine love.

Life is a current, a river flowing down from great heights, from the unique Source. And this river of life is Christ Himself. This is why Jesus proclaimed, 'I am the way and the truth and the life.' Can you tell me why an Initiate who hears these words immediately sees a picture in his mind of a river flowing from the mountains to the sea? The way, the truth, the life. What do these three words mean? The way is the riverbed, the channel in which the water flows. Life is the water itself, flowing in the river-bed. Truth is the spring from which the water flows and from which flows all creation. But there are even more profound meanings to be found in this image: the river-bed, with all its meanderings is the path of wisdom tracing its way back to the source: Truth. And the water is love and also life, for life is none other than love: life is born of love. Water is the symbol of both life and love. All the currents of energy, all the forces flowing through the cosmos are pictured as water, the life-giving fluid which irrigates the earth and slakes the thirst of all creatures.

So that is what Jesus meant, 'I am the path of wisdom, I am the love which gives birth to divine life, I am the fountainhead of truth from which flows the River of Life to quench the thirst of all creatures.' Get into the habit, therefore, of directing your thoughts to the pure, translucent waters of this spring. Never let a day go by without drinking deeply of the only water that can quench your thirst. Linger by this pure spring for as long as possible and you will begin to understand the secrets of life.

Chapter 11

THE NEW JERUSALEM: PERFECTED MAN

I

The Gates

In the Book of Revelation St. John says, 'I saw the Holy City, the new Jerusalem, coming down out of heaven from God... It had a great, high wall with twelve gates, and with twelve angels at the gates. On the gates were written the names of the twelve tribes of Israel. There were three gates on the east, three on the north, three on the south and three on the west... The twelve gates were twelve pearls, each gate made of a single pearl.'

These words were written two thousand years ago and no one has yet seen a city coming down to earth from Heaven, and no one ever will; it is no use looking up to see if it is coming! Why should a city come down from Heaven? A single city for billions of people does not seem very adequate. And how could it land on earth without crushing a lot of poor people? What kind of cables would be strong enough to hold the weight of it ? No doubt, the very best and most highly skilled technicians from Heaven would be hired to do the job... You see what happens if you take a text from Scripture literally: it becomes ridiculous. In fact, the new Jerusalem is a symbol, a symbol of the new man of the future. So stop looking up to Heaven to see if the new Jerusalem is on its way and set to work to *become* that new Jerusalem with its twelve gates.

You will probably wonder, 'Why twelve gates?' and the answer is that the Holy City is built in the image of the universe and also in the image of man. For man was built with twelve gates or doors. What are our eyes? Two doors. And our ears? Two more doors. And our two nostrils? Two more doors giving entry to the two currents, Ida and Pingala. That makes six and if you add the mouth it makes seven. Two more doors can be seen on the breast. They are different from the doors on the head but they are still doors, although in men's bodies they have no active function. The tenth door is in the region of the solar plexus: it is the navel or umbilicus, through which woman transmits to the child in her womb the blood and all the elements it needs to grow and develop. As for the last two doors, I will leave you to find them for yourselves. So that makes twelve in all. To me it is a constant source of wonder to see how Nature has fashioned the human body with its twelve doors.

Now the function of a door is to allow passage from one place to another, if not for human beings, then for forces, currents or invisible entities. And although, at the moment, most people's doors function only on the physical level, the question is essential, for the time has come to open up the ears, the eyes, the nose and the mouth so that they function on the spiritual level as well. When one begins to be clairvoyant or clairaudient, when one begins to breathe the perfume and taste the savour of the celestial world, when one's word begins to be creative, it means that one has begun to open one's doors. But our doors can only be opened if we know how to purify ourselves.

St. John tells us that each of the twelve gates of the new Jerusalem was made of a single pearl. Here again it is symbolic, for what kind of oyster could ever produce such an enormous pearl? Esoteric Science tells us that a pearl symbolizes purity and is dedicated to the moon because, thanks to its emanations, it has a special relationship with the moon. There are many things that could be said about a pearl: it is interesting, for example, to see how an oyster produces a pearl, for it is not a spontaneous phenomenon of Nature, but the fruit of a deliberate action on the part of the oyster. The process starts when a grain of sand gets into the oyster's shell and causes irritation. As the oyster has no way of getting rid of the sand it has to find some way of getting rid of the difficulty it is causing. So it concentrates and meditates and ends by realizing that if it secretes a substance with which to surround and envelop the grain of sand it will no longer irritate. So it sets to work in harmony with the phases of the moon and, lo and behold, the hard, rough, irritating grain of sand becomes polished and satin-smooth! This is how the pearl oyster has learned to overcome its difficulties.

For thousands of years oysters have been demonstrating this, but human beings have such limited intelligence they have never understood! So what exactly is the lesson it holds for us? Just this: we, too, can transform all the difficulties and obstacles we meet in life into pearls and precious stones. Suppose you are faced with some big problem: you cannot get rid of it and you cannot get around it, so now you must set to work and change it into a pearl. Whenever a difficulty arises, throw some tiny particles of love and intelligence over it and wrap it in purity and light. Just think of the wealth you can accumulate, all the pearls you can make, simply by applying your intelligence, patience, willpower and perseverance and, above all, gratitude to your unwavering ideal. Why not get into the habit of enveloping all your difficulties, all the little things that bother you, in a luminous, irridescent covering? This is the best way to get rich. I wish you could understand this! You must transform all your difficulties, and even your enemies, into pearls of great price. Does this sound like pure fantasy? Possibly. But I assure you it is not: it is very true. So, stop complaining and rebelling against your lot, otherwise you will never learn to produce the magic that turns difficulties into pearls.

Now, before you can begin something you have never done before, you must understand just what it involves. In the first place you must open yourself to the four points of the compass: these four points form a cross and in each branch of the cross there are three doors. When you open your twelve doors you establish contact with the cosmic forces of light, and it is thanks to these forces that you can transform the very nature of your being. Once reborn, purified, sanctified and illumined, you become the new Jerusalem, lit by the indwelling sun. So, set to work and with the means and methods provided by our Teaching, you will achieve a total transformation of your own material, making it pliant, expressive and radiant. This is what it means to open your doors and let in the light so that God Himself may dwell in you.

Up to now we know only the physical function of the twelve doors in our bodies; we still have to discover their spiritual function. Take the example of one of the doors in a man's body: we all know that it serves two purposes, elimination and procreation, but Initiatic Science teaches that it has five other, still unknown, functions – which makes seven in all – and that can be used to resolve certain problems and accomplish certain special functions. Now, I know that you are thinking, 'Five unknown functions? Oh, this is fascinating. Tell us more! But it is still very difficult to talk about these things: most human beings have been indoctrinated with so many false notions that it would be dangerous to reveal certain very sacred truths to them at the moment. All I shall say, therefore, is that our twelve doors will, one day, enable both men and women to accomplish great things for, when Nature created them, she had ambitious plans in mind and she is only waiting for human beings to reach a sufficient degree of maturity before revealing these new possibilities. Men and women are unaware that they are in possession of the keys that could unlock all mysteries, that their organs will one day enable them to work great wonders. They still do not know how to set about it, but once they are ready and capable of understanding, all this will be revealed to them. Mankind is destined to attain a profound understanding of the twelve doors, to explore all their hidden potentialities and to bring to light the wealth they conceal.

When one speaks of a door, the notion of passage or access is always implied. Nobody builds a doorway for no purpose, if there is nothing on either side except in a stage set, of course. In principle, a door gives access to another place: a city, a palace or a temple. It may open on to fabulous treasures or on to visions of terror. A great many tales and legends speak of doors which have to be opened or, on the contrary, kept locked for fear of releasing all kinds of monsters which threaten the life of the hero. And it is true that there really are doors which must not be opened prematurely.

When men and women discover the five hidden functions of their sexual organs they will have the power to accomplish wonders but, for the time being, I am obliged to be silent on this subject. From time immemorial, Initiates have always drawn a veil of secrecy over these truths and if they taught that our 'private parts' should be covered it was not for reasons of modesty or hygiene. It was an indication that they were better concealed because they had too great a significance, too much power.

Doors, therefore, are extremely important symbols. You have often been surprised by my insistence that you must learn when to open and, above all, when to close the doors of your house and you have probably wondered why I should attach so much importance to such apparently insignificant details. But many accidents and mishaps occur because people do not know when to open and when to close, nor even what to open and what to close. If it were only a question of physical doors it would not matter so much, but there are other, non-physical doors, and it is those I want to talk about. Beyond the physical world I can see another world, and when I see that some of you always leave your physical doors open, without even being aware of it, I know that they leave their inner doors wide open too, so that all kinds of undesirable visitors and spirits go in and out as they please. They are not capable of safeguarding the spiritual treasures they have received. Everything is wide open, it is easy to despoil them.

Many of you complain that when you go home, after a time at the Bonfin or at Izgrev, you seem to lose your ardour and enthusiasm very quickly. The reason is simple: you don't know how to hold on to the spiritual light and warmth you received while you were here. You may ask, 'But how can I hang on to them for a long time?' And the answer is, 'By closing your doors.' If you lose all your inspiration so quickly it is because you are ignorant and don't know how to close your doors. They stay wide open and burglars come in and make off with everything.

There are so many things you never stop to think about! And yet, if there is a lot of noise going on in the room next door, you automatically close your own door to shut it out. On the physical plane you know what to do but on the astral plane you leave everything wide open and then wonder why you are distressed or fall ill. It is a very vast question, this question of doors! Your hearts and minds are doors, too, and as you never know what you should let in or whom you should keep out, you let in all kinds of insignificant or infamous people and you shut the door on the Lord!

All of life is based on these two movements: opening and closing. This is what oysters and other molluscs teach us and we must learn to observe and understand. Shellfish which open and close teach us that life is an alternation of opening and closing. It is essential, therefore, to know when to open and when to close, otherwise we shall never obtain the purity of a pearl.

St. John also mentions that at each gate of the new Jerusalem there was an angel. Yes, every man and woman who is so pure as to become the new Jerusalem has an angel at each door, with the special task of receiving and transforming whatever enters. An angel admits what you hear, see, breathe, eat, and so on, and transforms it. So, when a truly pure woman conceives, an angel works on the seed in her womb so that the child will be born a genius or a divinity. But when a woman is impure, a demon lies in wait behind her door and she will give birth to an idiot or a monster.

There are so many more things to reveal to you but be patient! It will all come one day. You still do not know what men and women really are, how they are constructed, what forces are at work in them and how they should live in order to become tabernacles of the living God, new Jerusalems. For years, now, I have been leading you towards the day when each one of you will become a new Jerusalem.

II

The Foundations

From earliest antiquity men have believed that precious stones were endowed with marvellous powers and were symbols of heavenly virtues.

In the Old Testament we read that Moses' brother, Aaron, who had been chosen to minister to the Lord as High Priest, received priestly vestments which included the breastplate, a square of linen set with four rows of precious stones. The first row consisted of a sardius, a topaz and a carbuncle; the second row included an emerald, a sapphire and a diamond; the third included an opal, a jacinth and an amethyst, and the fourth row consisted of a beryl, an onyx and a jasper. Twelve stones in all.

And St. John, in the Book of Revelation, describes the Heavenly Jerusalem as a square city set on twelve foundations of precious stones. The first foundation was jasper, the second sapphire, the third chalcedony, the fourth emerald, the fifth sardonyx, the sixth cornelian, the seventh chrysolite, the eighth beryl, the ninth topaz, the tenth chrysoprase, the eleventh jacinth and the twelfth amethyst.

The reason why precious stones are so valuable is that they represent the purest quintessence of the earth. They are the end result of a long process of transformation carried out by the earth working on the raw materials of which it is composed. With great science and tremendous patience, the earth has managed to transform that matter, to 'ripen' it and change it into precious stones: rubies, turquoises, emeralds, sapphires and diamonds. What does anyone know about the earth? No one realizes that it is a living, intelligent being with a soul and a spirit and that it is continually hard at work.

The earth prepares all these treasures in its underground workshops for only one reason: it has the overwhelming desire to materialize the qualities and virtues of the heavenly realms. The earth wants to reflect and manifest these virtues, here below, in concrete, tangible form. And it is up to us, human beings, to imitate the earth and undertake the task of transforming our own raw materials into precious stones, that is, into virtues. The custom of putting precious stones on priestly robes or the crowns of kings comes from the knowledge that they symbolize the qualities and virtues of the most highly evolved beings. And the different stones represent different virtues: a topaz represents wisdom, a sapphire truth, a ruby love, and so on. And if the kings of this world wear precious stones in their crowns it is in imitation of the Creator, for the Creator wears a crown studded with innumerable precious, glittering gems: the virtues of the celestial hierarchies.

Human beings are always strongly attracted by precious stones and want to possess them because they feel, intuitively, that they represent something very valuable: heavenly virtues and qualities. But precious stones are a purely exterior manifestation of heavenly treasures. If you want to possess the spiritual qualities they represent, you have to extract them from the gems and let them penetrate your hearts and souls. The stones are merely material symbols which must be made to come alive, that is, they must become virtues in human souls. When men and women succeed in giving life to their own, inner gems, then they will become divinities.

There is nothing wrong in being attracted by gems and wanting to possess them. On the contrary, why should we despise or underestimate the value of elements which the earth and the stars have laboured to produce and in which God Himself has hidden great virtues and a mysterious science? It is normal to love and admire them but that does not mean that we should be ready to go to any lengths to possess them. All these things must be studied and understood and put in proper perspective so that we can use them for our own advancement and for the coming of God's Kingdom on earth. If we see things in their proper perspective we shall be stimulated and full of joy and wonderment, because then we shall see more clearly how God works in the universe. If someone loses all sense of proportion in this, and avidly collects precious stones in order to get rich or uses them to show off or seduce some poor creature, he deprives himself of the science inherent in them and, above all, of the wondrous joy of using them for spiritual purposes.

The job of the disciple is to become a precious stone, so lovely, pure and transparent that even God, looking down from Heaven, will be amazed and full of admiration and will send one of His servants down to earth, saying, 'Go and fetch that precious stone for me. I shall put it in my crown.' And, of course, in his endeavour to become a precious stone, the disciple is entitled to make use of the physical gems. There is no reason why a spiritual labour should not have a physical starting point, a material foundation on which to build; so a gem, for instance, can be used as a link with the spiritual reality it represents. Do not say, 'Oh, I am only interested in spiritual things. Material, physical things don't interest me.' That is the wrong attitude and it will not get you very far. Nature works with matter and man has no right to neglect it. It is there to instruct him and to point the way.

A precious stone, however small, is a particle of matter capable of picking up and retaining cosmic forces. It is this property which we have to learn to use. On the other hand, this does not mean that you can rely solely on the stone as though it could automatically transform or cure you and communicate its virtues to you. No. If you fail to do your share, if you do not work on the spiritual level, it is no use counting on your precious stone. It will be no use at all. Your stone is like an antenna: you can use it to transmit messages and it will be a faithful, hardworking servant who will carry out your orders, for behind its surface reality are vibrant, active forces.

In this, as in other areas, you can only work really effectively if you fully understand the tools you use. Otherwise it is simply superstition. People count on talismans and pentacles or on metal rings and bracelets and even on the roots of certain plants. And there is never any lack of crooks and frauds to make your mouth water with their tempting propositions, 'For only a small sum we'll send you that rarest of rarities, a mandrake root. Once you are in possession of this magic charm, the doors of treasure-houses and palaces will open before you as if by enchantment and beautiful women will fall into your arms.' You can imagine how this whets the appetite of a lot of stupid people who say to themselves, 'I'll get the mandrake and then love, money and freedom will be mine!' And do you know what they get in return for their money? A tiny wooden doll, carved to look like a mandrake root. Really, how can people be so gullible? But, enough of that; it is not a very interesting subject.

What is important is to know how to assess things at their true value. A gem will never do your share of the work. True, it has been prepared by Nature to receive and transmit certain cosmic energies, but it is no good putting your faith in your precious stone and then sitting back to wait for results! You have to use it explicitly, for a specific purpose, in accordance with its own specific properties, to help you acquire, for example, the virtues it symbolizes. But what is really important is that your stone become part of your inner self, that you plant it and cultivate it in your inner life. It is all very well to wear pearls and precious stones, but if you have not understood the spirit of this new Teaching and never try to form gems within yourself, you will not achieve anything by wearing them. The physical stone can be no more than a model to inspire you and show you how to reproduce it within yourself, like the models used by painters and sculptors. So, by all means, gaze at precious stones and admire them as much as you like but, above all, try to create them within yourself as living jewels. If you have the right attitude towards precious stones, then it is very useful to possess some, otherwise it is either vanity or superstition.

Has it ever occurred to you to wonder why gems are so sought after by men and women? It is because of the light they give off. Their vibrations are so perfectly synchronized with the forces of Nature that they have become transparent. They allow light to shine through them so that it can be seen in all its subtlest shades and nuances. A disciple of the New Life is also a precious stone. He knows that if he wants to be truly beautiful, he has to let the Lord, the Supreme Light, dwell in him and shine through him until even his physical body is resplendent with light.

For it is possible for the physical body to become light: Jesus demonstrated this in his transfiguration on Mount Thabor. The Gospels say that his face shone more brightly than the sun and his clothes became as white as light itself. It is important for you to realize that this kind of transfiguration is possible for all of us. All those who have managed to purify and sublimate their physical bodies can be transfigured, like Jesus. When someone works consciously and for a very long time, in faith, hope and love, his physical body becomes so sublimated and pure, all its particles vibrate with such intensity, that it can be transfigured just as Jesus' body was transfigured. And there you have the new Jerusalem!

The new Jerusalem is preparing for the day when it will come down from Heaven into this world. This means that the angels are with us, that they are at work in all those who have made up their minds to transform and purify themselves. Every day and every night, billions of drab, lifeless particles are discarded and replaced by others, ethereal, supple and luminous. Thousands of new Jerusalems are getting ready to form the one, great New Jerusalem in which God will dwell on earth.

Chapter 12

LEARNING TO READ AND WRITE

I

When you go out for a walk, do you ever think of picking up some of the stones or pebbles you see along the way and talking to them? I doubt it! And the reason is that you let yourselves be fooled by appearances: you think that stones are inanimate, that they have no souls. And yet you would be astonished at the tales they could tell you if only you knew how to listen to them. For everything that exists on earth is alive and the history of the universe is inscribed on rocks and pebbles, and on everything else in Nature. Yes, believe me: everything that has ever occurred is on record. Human beings are very presumptuous to think that it was they who first discovered how to record events. True, they have done wonders with photography, films, records, magnetic tape and so on. The only trouble is that it never occurs to them that they have managed to achieve so much only because the phenomenon of recording already exists in Nature: the whole of Nature is sensitive and reacts to events.

Some researchers in the United States, experimenting with highly specialized equipment, have determined that plants possess a sensitivity which makes them react to the presence of beneficial or harmful elements. They discovered that if someone who had previously ill-treated the plants approached them, they showed signs of 'fear'. So this also means that they have a memory. But if plants are sensitive, so are stones, in their own way. If you love them. if you touch them lovingly they are capable of responding and revealing their secrets to you.

Love is the language of the universe. The whole of Creation, every single creature. understands this language. Touch a stone lovingly and it will vibrate quite differently, and it can even respond with love. Only you have to be very sensitive to perceive this; you have to learn its language. But who wants to learn the language of stones, plants and animals? Human beings learn to read and write in all the languages of the world, except the language of Nature. And yet it is the only one worth knowing.

Although reading and writing have become indispensable skills in the civilized world of today it does not necessarily follow that man could not make progress without them. The capacity to read and write has many advantages, no doubt, but the tremendous importance given to pieces of paper has many disadvantages also. People put all their trust in pieces of paper, they are the only things that count. If a piece of paper says you are guilty, since nobody is capable of reading your innocence on your face, they will read the paper and, even if it is not true, put you in prison. Man counts for nothing any more. Paper is everything.

We are living in a civilization that requires that we know how to read and write. That is all well and good, but what I want to make abundantly clear to you is that there are other kinds of reading and writing. It will always be necessary to know how to read and write, but you have to be able to do so on different levels. For an Initiate, to read means to be able to decipher the subtle, secret dimensions of objects and of all living creatures, to interpret the signs and symbols traced by Cosmic Intelligence on every page of the great Book of the Universe. And to write is to put one's mark on that book, to act upon minerals and plants, animals and men, by the magic power of one's spirit. So it is not only on paper that we have to learn to read and write, but in all regions of the universe.

I have sometimes said to people with university degrees, professors and scholars, that they have not yet even begun. 'What do you mean, we haven't begun?' 'It's true. You can't even read or write! "You can't be serious! Read and write indeed! Of course we can read and write. "No. None of the things you read is of any importance. What you should be doing is reading the living Book of Nature. Are you capable of reading that book? And as for writing, do you know how to write divine words on the souls, hearts and minds of men?'

Just take the example of a man who uses his pen to write in a woman's 'book': the result is a sickly, ailing child, probably a future criminal. What better proof do you want that that man did not know how to write?

The second card of the Tarot portrays Pope Joan, a seated woman with a formidable expression of power and authority, holding an open book in her lap. The book is, in fact, a symbol of the female sexual organs. And men write in the book with their 'pens'. The book, of course, is purely passive and once something has been written on it, it will never be effaced. So it is important that the writer be intelligent and know what he is writing. If he is a fool, a weakling or a drunkard, how can he write something beautiful, meaningful, profound or intelligent? The child – for his writing represents the child – will be crippled, unhealthy and unbalanced.

In the past it was very difficult to persuade parents to send their children to school. They could not see what good it would do them to learn to read and write when they had to take care of the livestock and plough the land. And now, what a difference! All children in the world, almost, go to school. Even the most primitive people understand that it is useful. But just as it was difficult, in the past, to persuade people that they needed instruction, it is going to be equally difficult now, to teach them what reading and writing really means and to persuade them to practise it.

Human beings are illiterate; they are incapable of reading the great Book of Nature and finding the solutions to their problems in it. They readily consult books by famous authors in which they find all kinds of contradictory answers to their questions, but never do they consult Nature herself, who solved all life's problems aeons ago. Yes, the solutions to your problems are all there, in the mineral, vegetable and animal worlds and even in man himself, in the way he is built and in the different functions of his body.

Human beings cannot read, and neither can they write. Oh, of course, they do write because every thought and every feeling is a manner of writing and it is all recorded somewhere, on material objects or in the minds and hearts of men and women. But this is just scribbling and it serves no useful purpose for anyone.

Writing is an act of the will and it requires sacrifice. To write is to awaken and harness inner forces and to express them outwardly in the act of giving them to another human being. To write is also to leave traces of oneself and many philosophers and artists have left traces which are still being studied today, thousands of years after they have gone. But on a much higher level than artists and philosophers are the great Initiates, veritable creators who work with the forces of divine magic. He who knows how to work with divine magic has only to trace a few words in space, in letters of fire, and his words speed through the air, etching themselves into the minds and hearts of men and women everywhere.

Every living being is also a book. A book which each one of us is in the process of writing. But what gibberish it often is! What a hodgepodge of discordant notes! Every conceivable anomaly and aberration can be found in human books, and when two such books meet and fall head over heals in love they spend their days and nights 'reading' each other. And what do they learn from their reading? All too often they learn of hellish things, for human beings are still not aware that they are the authors of their own books.

Up to now they have only learned to work on objects exterior to themselves. Their inner landscape is still an untamed wilderness. And this is true even for artists. Artists create beauty, but the beauty they create is always external to themselves because they never work on their own materials. One day, since they are purely external, all their creations will disappear and when they return to earth in later reincarnations, they will have to begin all over again. Whereas a true painter, sculptor or poet, a true musician, works on himself and will never be separated from his paintings, sculptures, books or symphonies. He will take them with him when he leaves this world and bring them back again, within himself, in his next incarnation. This is true evolution.

I do not deny that artists have left many immortal masterpieces which continue to inspire the whole of mankind and contribute to its evolution, but according to the teachings of Initiatic Science, according to Cosmic Intelligence, which has revealed to me the goal and purpose of creation, this is not enough. There are higher degrees of art. I have immense admiration for the great cathedrals, symphonies and sculptures of the world, but the true ideal is to create such splendours inside oneself, to be one's own painting, one's own statue, poem, music or dance. You will, perhaps, object, 'But then no one else would benefit from your works of art,' and that is where you are mistaken. The true instructors of mankind who created themselves, who wrote and carved themselves, have always caused upheavals affecting the entire planet, simply by the fact of their presence. All the shapes and colours, all the poetry and music of the world could be seen and heard, flowing through them. A human being who is his own creation, his own work of art, does far more for humanity than all libraries, museums and masterpieces of the world because these are all dead, whereas he is alive!

II

Wherever you tread, whatever you touch, you leave behind you a trace, an imprint which may be beneficial or it may be harmful. Some people are so full of venom that, as the saying goes, 'the grass will never grow again where they have trod': this is no exaggeration. There are others, on the contrary, who are so bent on helping and liberating their fellow men, on bringing life, light and warmth to all creatures, that they leave imprints of great power for good which influence all those who come after them.

Knowing the existence and the potency of these phenomena, I have conducted many an interesting experiment, things of which you can have no inkling. Whenever I travel on the seas and oceans of the world I make contact with the powers which govern these regions, imploring them to be favourable to all those who sail across their waters or bathe along their beaches and to give them the graces of brotherliness and divine light. I write out certain formulae and throw the messages into the sea, and as the creatures of these regions are very advanced, very highly conscious and sensitive beings, I know that my messages are well received and acted upon. We are all capable of changing things in the world but if we want to understand how to set about it, we have to be conscious of the more subtle dimensions of matter. For quite some time now, experiments have been going on in this field, particularly in the United States and in Russia: scientists are beginning to study the subtler emanations of men, animals, plants, even inanimate objects, all those phenomena which they consider to be 'para-psychical'. Unfortunately, these extraordinary discoveries may well lead mankind ever nearer the brink of catastrophe, for human nature is such that men tend to use every new discovery to satisfy their own selfish interests and whims or their thirst for domination and revenge.

All this knowledge, therefore, is in danger of being used primarily to the detriment of others; in fact this is already the case: gifts impregnated with malevolent influences have been sent to world leaders with the intention of injuring them. Of course, this can be most effective, but it is black magic and anyone who uses black magic should know that one day, sooner or later, they will be punished for it. For the laws are adamant: whatever you give to others, whether good or evil, always bounces back and, in fact, it comes back amplified. So, if what you have sent out is evil: beware! Magic must be used exclusively to help human beings and to spread light and peace throughout the world. If this is your intention you will have your name inscribed in Heaven amongst the workers of white magic and you will bring abundant blessings on yourself.

So, wherever you go, think of doing something positive by your power of thought, for when you do so the thousands of intelligent creatures who surround you will be aware of it. You may say, 'But I can't see these creatures.' That is no argument; they do exist. And if you learn to work with the invisible, subtler dimensions of reality you will be capable of producing wonderful changes for the better throughout the entire world. This law is as true as any of the laws of physics and chemistry. The room in which you live, its walls and all the furniture and other objects in it, bear fluidic traces of your presence, and if a highly sensitive medium were to come and see you and touch some object in your room, he would be able to feel and describe to you, in detail, all that has ever occurred in that room.

Even with a single hair from your head a clairvoyant can give you a detailed description of your character and health, your vices and virtues. How is it possible that all this can be recorded in one hair? Well, it is. That is all I can say. You have probably heard of that remarkable Bulgarian clairvoyant, Vanga, but do you know how she operates? She asks the person who wants to consult her to give her a lump of sugar he has held in his hand for a few moments. So even from another country you can get someone to take her the lump of sugar, and Vanga – who is blind, incidentally, like so many other great clairvoyants – simply picks it up and, from it, reads your character and all your past, present and future. The trace you left on the sugar is weightless, and yet it is enough for her. She can read in it everything about you. But people with such astonishing gifts of mediumship are very rare nowadays. In the past, magicians prepared extremely powerful talismans, thanks to their understanding of these influences. But over the course of centuries human beings have more and more lost touch with the invisible world.

Once you have understood this law, that everything you do, think, say or feel is recorded, then you must take care to utter only words of prayer and good wishes wherever you go. 'May all who come this way be touched by the forces of light, kindness and brotherliness. May their lives be transformed.' Why not get into the habit of pronouncing blessings like this along your way? When it comes to curses there are always plenty of candidates ready and willing, but for blessings? Suppose you go for a stroll in the woods, for instance, why not pray that all those who go through those woods in the future become better people, children of God, working for peace?

You will probably tell me that no one has ever talked to you about this kind of thing before. But why should you need anyone to tell you? When you have a baby of your own, or someone you love very much, do you need anyone to suggest that you wish him all kinds of blessings? No, you do so spontaneously because it comes from the heart, your feelings urge you to express certain wishes and pronounce certain words. So why not do the same, spontaneously, for the whole world? Look at how people behave when they travel: either they do nothing but amuse themselves or they are bored to tears. Wouldn't it be splendid if they learned to work mentally so as to be able to help all the people living in the areas they are travelling through, and all future travellers?

Now, some of you may ask, 'But do we have any right to go about influencing Nature and leaving our imprints on it?' What a question! Most human beings spend their time soiling and spoiling Nature with the black magic of their negative thoughts and feelings, and we, don't we have the right to work for light, peace and brotherhood? Strange reasoning indeed! Has anyone ever questioned the rose's right to perfume the air? Of course you have the right to act upon and influence the whole of Nature, but on one condition: that you leave only beneficial, luminous imprints wherever you go, so that people who come that way after you, may receive particles that will help them to think better, to feel better, to act better.

Similarly, if you travel by ship on a lake, the sea or a river, you can write a note and address it to the entity who has dominion over the waters. Your prayer will receive attention and thousands of creatures will set to work to answer it. Anybody can do this, anyone can formulate prayers for the world, but only someone who is very advanced will get great results. His prayers will be answered because of his light and purity, because of his great worth. Your work in the invisible world will get results in proportion to your preparedness: it will be productive if it is backed up by qualities and virtues. And this holds good for what concerns talismans, also. Many people buy and wear a talisman under the illusion that it will automatically bring them success in all their undertakings. Not so! Even a talisman prepared especially for you by a great magician will not help you for long unless you, yourself, put life into it and nourish it with your thoughts and feelings and the purity of your life. Otherwise, after a while, it will simply lose all its power and die. No talisman can be made to last eternally. Its life depends on the person who wears it.

You must get into the habit, therefore, of saying and even of writing words of blessing. When we are together you have often seen me writing something on a piece of paper. Today, for the first time, I shall tell you what I write: it is a prayer, 'May Thy name, Oh Lord, be blessed and hallowed for all eternity.' But I write it in Bulgarian, *'Da beudé blagoslovéno i svéto Iméto v'véka, Gospodi'*, because that is how I used to say it in Bulgaria when I was young. And why, you may wonder, do I do this? I do it because it does me good! And you can do the same, all day long: think of blessing God's name say it out loud or write it down. Of course, God's name is already blessed by the angels. What you do will not add very much to the holiness of God's name! But it will do you a power of good and others, too, for the sacred words will purify the atmosphere around them. And if you are wondering whether this can make any lasting impression, the answer is that it all depends on the intensity of your thought and the firmness of your will.

Today you have learned a lot of truths that are new to you. If you try to apply them to your lives, you will notice an improvement in all areas, for only truths such as these can bring light into everything you do and vivify and resuscitate everything within you.

By the same author:
(Translated from the French)

Izvor Collection

201 – Toward a Solar Civilization
202 – Man, Master of his Destiny
203 – Education Begins Before Birth
204 – The Yoga of Nutrition
205 – Sexual Force or the Winged Dragon
206 – A Philosophy of Universality
207 – What is a Spiritual Master?
208 – Under the Dove, the Reign of Peace
209 – Christmas and Easter in the Initiatic Tradition
210 – The Tree of the Knowledge of Good and Evil
211 – Freedom, the Spirit Triumphant
212 – Light is a Living Spirit
213 – Man's Two Natures: Human and Divine
214 – Hope for the World: Spiritual Galvanoplasty
215 – The True Meaning of Christ's Teaching
216 – The Living Book of Nature
217 – New Light on the Gospels
218 – The Symbolic Language of Geometrical Figures
219 – Man's Subtle Bodies and Centres
220 – The Zodiac, Key to Man and to the Universe
221 – True Alchemy or the Quest for Perfection
222 – Man's Psychic Life: Elements and Structures
223 – Creation: Artistic and Spiritual
224 – The Powers of Thought
225 – Harmony and Health
226 – The Book of Divine Magic
227 – Golden Rules for Everyday Life
228 – Looking into the Invisible
229 – The Path of Silence
230 – The Book of Revelations: a Commentary
231 – The Seeds of Happiness
232 – The Mysteries of Fire and Water
233 – Youth: Creators of the Future
234 – Truth, Fruit of Wisdom and Love
235 – 'In Spirit and in Truth'
236 – Angels and other Mysteries of The Tree of Life
237 – Cosmic Balance, The Secret of Polarity
238 – The Faith That Moves Mountains
239 – Love Greater Than Faith

Books by Omraam Mikhaël Aïvanhov
(translated from the French)

Complete Works

Volume 1 – The Second Birth
Volume 2 – Spiritual Alchemy
Volume 5 – Life Force
Volume 6 – Harmony
Volume 7 – The Mysteries of Yesod
Volume 10 – The Splendour of Tiphareth
The Yoga of the Sun
Volume 11 – The Key to the Problems of Existence
Volume 12 – Cosmic Moral Laws
Volume 13 – A New Earth
Methods, Exercises, Formulas, Prayers
Volume 14 – Love and Sexuality (Part I)
Volume 15 – Love and Sexuality (Part II)
Volume 17 – 'Know Thyself' Jnana Yoga (Part I)
Volume 18 – 'Know Thyself' Jnana Yoga (Part II)
Volume 25 – A New Dawn:
Society and Politics in the Light of Initiatic Science (Part I)
Volume 26 – A New Dawn:
Society and Politics in the Light of Initiatic Science (Part II)
Volume 29 – On the Art of Teaching (Part III)
Volume 30 – Life and Work in an Initiatic School
Training for the Divine
Volume 32 – The Fruits of the Tree of Life
The Cabbalistic Tradition

Brochures:

301 – The New Year
302 – Meditation
303 – Respiration
304 – Death and the Life Beyond

By the same author:

Daily Meditations:
A thought for each day of the year
A volume published every year

Life Recordings on Tape
KC2510 AN – The Laws of Reincarnation
(Two audio cassettes)

Videos (french/english)

V 4605 FR – *The Activity of the Soul and Spirit:*
How They Can Manifest Through Us.
How Can We Modify our Destiny?
L'activité de l'âme et de l'esprit et notre travail
pour qu'ils se manifestent à travers nous.
Comment peut-on changer sa destinée?

V 4606 FR – *How Can We Purify our Physical Body*
Despite the Pollution of the Atmosphere and Food?
Comment peut-on purifier le corps physique
malgré la pollution de l'air et de la nourriture?

World Wide - Editor-Distributor

Editions PROSVETA S.A. - B.P. 12 - F- 83601 Fréjus Cedex (France)

Tel. (00 33) 04 94 19 33 33 - Fax (00 33) 04 94 19 33 34

Web: **www.prosveta.com**

e-mail: **international@prosveta.com**

Distributors

AUSTRALASIA

Australia - New Zealand - Hong Kong - Taïwan - Singapore
SURYOMA LTD - P.O. Box 2218 – Bowral – N.S.W. 2576 Australia
e-mail: info@suryoma.com – Tel. (61) 2 4872 3999 – fax (61) 2 4872 4022

AUSTRIA

HARMONIEQUELL VERSAND – A- 5302 Henndorf am Wallersee, Hof 37
Tel. / fax (43) 6214 7413 – e-mail: info@prosveta.at

BELGIUM & LUXEMBOURG

PROSVETA BENELUX – Liersesteenweg 154 B-2547 Lint
Tel (32) 3/455 41 75 – Fax 3/454 24 25 – e-mail: prosveta@skynet.be
N.V. MAKLU Somersstraat 13-15 – B-2000 Antwerpen
Tel. (32) 3/231 29 00 – Fax 3/233 26 59
VANDER S.A. – Av. des Volontaires 321 – B-1150 Bruxelles
Tel. (32) 27 62 98 04 – Fax 27 62 06 62

BULGARIA

SVETOGLED – Bd Saborny 16 A, appt 11 – 9000 Varna
e-mail: svetgled@revolta.com – Tel/Fax: (359) 52 23 98 02

CANADA

PROSVETA Inc. – 3950, Albert Mines – North Hatley (Qc), J0B 2C0
Tel. (819) 564-8212 – Fax. (819) 564-1823
in Canada, call toll free: 1-800-854-8212
e-mail: prosveta@prosveta-canada.com / www.prosveta-canada.com

COLUMBIA

PROSVETA – Calle 146 # 25-28 Apto 404 Int.2 – Bogotá
e-mail: kalagiya@tutopia.com

CYPRUS

THE SOLAR CIVILISATION BOOKSHOP – BOOKBINDING
73 D Kallipoleos Avenue - Lycavitos – P. O. Box 24947, 1355 – Nicosia
Tel / Fax 00357-2-377503

CZECH REPUBLIC

PROSVETA – Ant. Sovy 18, –České Budejovice 370 05
Tel / Fax: (420) 38-53 00 227 – e-mail: prosveta@iol.cz

GERMANY

PROSVETA Deutschland – Heer Strasse 55 – 78616 Rottweil
Tel. (49) 741-46551 – Fax. (49) 741-46552 – e-mail: prosveta.de@t-online.de
EDIS GmbH, Mühlweg 2 – 82054 Sauerlach
Tel. (49) 8104-6677-0 – Fax.(49) 8104-6677-99

GREAT BRITAIN – IRELAND

PROSVETA – The Doves Nest, Duddleswell Uckfield, – East Sussex TN 22 3JJ
Tel. (44) (01825) 712988 - Fax (44) (01825) 713386
e-mail: prosveta@pavilion.co.uk

GREECE

RAOMRON – D. RAGOUSSIS
3, rue A. Papamdreou – C.P. 16675 – Glifada - Athenes
Tel / Fax: (010) 9681127 – e-mail: raomron@hol.gr

HAITI

PROSVETA – DÉPÔT – B.P. 115, Jacmel, Haiti (W.I.)
Tel./ Fax (509) 288-3319
e-mail: uwbhaiti@citeweb.net

HOLLAND

STICHTING PROSVETA NEDERLAND
Zeestraat 50 – 2042 LC Zandvoort – e-mail: prosveta@worldonline.nl

ISRAEL

Zohar, P. B. 1046, Netanya 42110
e-mail: zohar@wanadoo.fr

ITALY

PROSVETA Coop. – Casella Postale – 06060 Moiano (PG)
Tel. (39) 075-8358498 – Fax 075-8359712
e-mail: prosveta@tin.it

LIBAN

PROSVETA LIBAN – P.O. Box 90-995
Jdeidet-el-Metn, Beirut – Tel. (03) 448560
e-mail : prosvetaliban@hotmail.com

NORWAY

PROSVETA NORDEN – Postboks 5101 – 1503 Moss
Tel. (47) 69 26 51 40 – Fax (47) 69 25 06 76
e-mail: prosveta Norden - prosnor@online.no

PORTUGAL & BRAZIL

EDIÇÕES PROSVETA – Rua Passos Manuel, n° 20 – 3e E, P 1150 – Lisboa
Tel. (351) (21) 354 07 64
PUBLICAÇÕES EUROPA-AMERICA Ltd
Est Lisboa-Sintra KM 14 – 2726 Mem Martins Codex
e-mail : prosvetapt@hotmail.com

ROMANIA

ANTAR – Str. N. Constantinescu 10 - Bloc 16A - sc A - Apt. 9,
Sector 1 – 71253 Bucarest
Tel. (40) 1 679 52 48 - Tel./ Fax (40) 1 231 37 19
e-mail : antared@pcnet.ro

RUSSIA

EDITIONS PROSVETA
Riazanski Prospekt 8a, office 407 – 109428 Moscou
Tel / Fax (7095) 232 08 79 – e-mail : prosveta@online.ru

SPAIN

ASOCIACIÓN PROSVETA ESPAÑOLA – C/ Ausias March n° 23 Ático
SP-08010 Barcelona – Tel (34) (3) 412 31 85 - Fax (34) (3) 302 13 72
aprosveta@prosveta.es

SWITZERLAND

PROSVETA Société Coopérative – CH - 1808 Les Monts-de-Corsier
Tel. (41) 21 921 92 18 – Fax. (41) 21 922 92 04
e-mail: prosveta@swissonline.ch

UNITED STATES

PROSVETA U.S.A. – P.O. Box 1176 – New Smyrna Beach, FL.32170-1176
Tel / Fax (386) 428-1465
e-mail: prosveta@prosveta-usa.com – web page: www.prosveta-usa.com

VENEZUELA

PROSVETA VENEZUELA C. A. – Calle Madrid
Quinta Monteserino – D. F. Las Mercedes – Caracas
Tel. (58) 0414 22 36 748 – e-mail : miguelclavijo@hotmail.com

Achevé d'imprimer en mai 2002
sur les presses de l'Imprimerie HEMISUD
83160 – La Valette-du-Var (France)

Dépôt légal : mai 2002
1er dépôt légal dans la même collection : 1984